The Origin of Capitalism

The Origin of Capitalism

Ellen Meiksins Wood

Monthly Review Press
New York

Library of Congress Cataloging-in-Publication Data
Wood, Ellen Meiksins.
    The origin of capitalism / Ellen Meiksins Wood.
        p.   cm.
    Includes bibliographical references and index.
    ISBN 1-58367-000-9 (pbk.)—ISBN 1-58367-007-6 (cloth)
    1. Capitalism--History.   I. Title.
  HB501.W615 1999
  330.12'2'09--dc21   98-48940
                                                 CIP

Monthly Review Press
122 West 27th Street
New York NY 10001

Manufactured in Canada
10 9 8 7 6 5 4 3 2 1

Contents

Acknowledgments

PARTS OF THIS BOOK HAVE APPEARED BEFORE, IN VARIOUS places: "From Opportunity to Imperative: The History of the Market," *Monthly Review* 46 (July-August 1994); "Capitalism, Merchants and Bourgeois Revolution: Reflections on the Brenner Debate and Its Sequel," *International Review of Social History* 41 (1996); "Modernity, Postmodernity, or Capitalism?" *Monthly Review* 48 (July-August 1996), which appeared in substantially revised and enlarged versions in *Review of International Political Economy* 41 (autumn 1997), and in Robert McChesney, John Bellamy Foster, and Ellen Meiksins Wood, eds., *Capitalism and the Information Age* (New York: Monthly Review Press, 1997); "The Non-History of Capitalism," *Historical Materialism* 1 (1997); Ellen Meiksins Wood and Neal Wood, *A Trumpet of Sedition; Political Theory and the Rise of Capitalism, 1509-1688* (New York: New York University Press, 1997); and "The Agrarian Origins of Capitalism," *Monthly Review* 50 (July-August 1998).

I want to thank Neal Wood for his comments and encouragement, and especially Chris Phelps, editorial director of Monthly Review Press, who not only persuaded me to produce this book but went well beyond routine editorial fine-tuning with his extremely useful and insightful criticisms and suggestions.

Finally, my thanks to the wonderful MRP staff, for everything they have done and are doing to produce and promote this book.

Introduction

THE COLLAPSE OF COMMUNISM IN THE LATE 1980s AND 1990s seemed to confirm what many people have long believed: that capitalism is the natural condition of humanity, that it conforms to the laws of nature and basic human inclinations, and that any deviation from those natural laws and inclinations can only come to grief.

There are, of course, many reasons today for questioning the capitalist triumphalism that followed in the wake of the collapse. As I write this introduction, my morning newspaper speaks of "perhaps the most serious breakdown in the modern capitalist era" and warns of a possible world depression on the scale of the 1930s and even wider in scope. The world is still reeling from the Asian crisis, and no one can doubt that we are a long way from the end of it, that its full effects on the global economy are yet to come. Meanwhile, the proudest accomplishment of capitalist triumph, the end of the Soviet Union, has led to the near-total collapse of the Russian economy, with wide-ranging effects throughout the advanced capitalist world—more damaging effects, some editorials in the Western press have said, than the Soviet Union ever inflicted on capitalism.

In the past, capitalism has always pulled out of its recurrent crises, but never without laying a foundation for new and even worse ones. The system will no doubt be salvaged from the wreckage this time, too. But whatever means are found to limit or correct the damage, it is certain that just as many millions of people will suffer from the cure as from the disease.

The increasingly transparent weaknesses and contradictions in the capitalist system may eventually convince even some of its more uncritical supporters that an alternative needs to be found. But the conviction that there is and can be no alternative is very deeply rooted, especially in Western culture. That conviction is supported not only by the more blatant expressions of capitalist ideology but also by some of our most cherished and unquestioned beliefs about history. It is as if capitalism has always been the destination of historical movement and, even more, that the movement of history itself has from the beginning been driven by capitalist "laws of motion."

Begging the Question

Capitalism is a system in which goods and services, down to the most basic necessities of life, are produced for profitable exchange, where even human labor power is a commodity for sale in the market, and where, because all economic actors are dependent on the market, the requirements of competition and profit maximization are the fundamental rules of life. Because of those rules, it is a system uniquely driven to develop the forces of production and to improve the productivity of labor by technical means. Above all, it is a system in which the bulk of society's work is done by propertyless laborers who are obliged to sell their labor power in exchange for a wage in order to gain access to the means of life. In the process of supplying the needs and wants of society, workers at the same time create profits for those who buy their labor power. In fact, the production of goods and services is subordinate to the production of capital and capitalist profit. The basic objective of the capitalist system, in other words, is the production and self-expansion of capital.

This distinctive way of supplying the material needs of human beings, so very different from all preceding ways of organizing material life and social reproduction, has existed for a very short time, barely a fraction of humanity's existence on earth. Even those who most emphatically insist on the system's roots in human nature would not claim that it existed before the early modern period, and then only in Western Europe. They may see hints of it in earlier periods, or detect its beginnings in the Middle Ages as a looming threat to a declining feudalism though it was still constrained by feudal restrictions, or say that it began with the expansion of trade or with voyages of discovery—in particular, Columbus's at the end of the fifteenth century. But few would say it existed in earnest before the sixteenth or seventeenth century, and some would place its arrival as late as the eighteenth century, or perhaps even the nineteenth, when it matured into its industrial form.

Yet historical accounts of how this system came into being have typically treated it as the natural realization of ever-present tendencies. Since historians first began explaining the emergence of capitalism, there has scarcely existed an explanation that did not begin by assuming the very thing that needed to be explained. Almost without exception, accounts of the origin of capitalism have been fundamentally circular: they have assumed the prior existence of capitalism in order to explain its coming into being. In order to explain capitalism's distinctive drive to maximize profit, they have presupposed the existence of a universal profit-maximizing rationality. In order to explain capitalism's drive to improve labor productivity by technical means, they have presupposed a continuous, almost natural, progress of technological improvement in the productivity of labor.

These question-begging explanations have their origins in classical political economy and Enlightenment conceptions of progress. Together, they give an account of historical development in which the emergence and growth to maturity of capitalism were already prefigured in the earliest manifestations of human rationality, in the technological advances that began when homo sapiens first wielded a tool, and in the acts of exchange human beings have practiced since time immemorial. History's journey to "commercial society" or capitalism, has, they admit, been long and arduous, and many obstacles have stood in its way. But its progress has nonetheless been natural and inevitable. Nothing more is required, then, to explain the "rise of capitalism" than an account of how the many obstacles to its forward movement have been lifted—sometimes gradually, sometimes suddenly, with revolutionary violence.

In most accounts of capitalism and its origin, there really *is* no origin. Capitalism seems always to *be* there, somewhere, and it only needs to be released from its chains—for instance, from the fetters of feudalism—to be allowed to grow and mature. Typically, these fetters are political: the parasitic powers of lordship, or the restrictions of an autocratic state. Sometimes they are cultural or ideological—perhaps the wrong religion. These constraints confine the free movement of economic actors, the free expression of economic rationality. The "economic" in these formulations is identified with exchange or markets, and it is here that we can detect the assumption that the seeds of capitalism are contained in the most simple acts of exchange, in any form of trade or market activity. That assumption is typically connected with the other presupposition, that history has been an almost natural process of technological development. One way or another, capitalism more or less naturally appears when and where expanding markets and technological development reach the right level. Many Marxist explanations are fundamentally the same—with the addition of bourgeois revolutions to help break the fetters.

The effect of these explanations is to stress the *continuity* between non-capitalist and capitalist societies, and to deny or disguise the *specificity* of capitalism. Exchange has existed more or less forever, and it seems that the capitalist market is just more of the same. In this kind of argument, because capitalism's specific and unique need to revolutionize the forces of production constantly is just an extension and an acceleration of universal, transhistorical, almost *natural* tendencies, industrialization is the inevitable outcome of humanity's most basic inclinations. So the lineage of capitalism passes naturally from the earliest Babylonian or Roman merchant through the medieval burgher to the early modern bourgeois and finally to the industrial capitalist.[1]

There is a similar logic in certain Marxist versions of this story, even though the narrative in more recent versions often shifts from the town to the countryside, and merchants are replaced by rural commodity producers, small or "middling" farmers seemingly waiting for the opportunity to blossom into full-blown capitalists. In this kind of narrative petty commodity production, released from the bonds of feudalism, grows more or less naturally into capitalism, and petty commodity producers, just given the chance, will take the capitalist road.

Central to these conventional accounts of history are certain assumptions, explicit or implicit, about human nature and about how human beings will behave, if only given the chance. They will, the story goes, always avail themselves of the opportunity to maximize profit through acts of exchange, and in order to realize that natural inclination, they will always find ways of improving the organization and instruments of work in order to enhance the productivity of labor.

Opportunity or Imperative?

In the classic model, then, capitalism is an opportunity to be taken, wherever and whenever possible. This notion of *opportunity* is absolutely critical to the conventional understanding of the capitalist system, present even in our everyday language. Consider common usage of the word that lies at the very heart of capitalism:

"market." Almost every definition of *market* in the dictionary connotes an *opportunity:* as a concrete locale or institution, a market is a place where opportunities exist to buy and sell; as an abstraction, a market is the possibility of sale. Goods "find a market," and we say there is a market for a service or commodity when there is a demand for it, which means it can and will be sold. Markets are "opened" to those who want to sell. The market represents "conditions as regards, opportunity for, buying and selling" *(The Concise Oxford Dictionary).* The market implies *offering* and *choice.*

What, then, are market *forces?* Doesn't force imply coercion? In capitalist ideology, the market implies not compulsion but freedom. At the same time, this freedom is guaranteed by certain mechanisms that ensure a rational economy, where supply meets demand, putting on offer commodities and services that people will freely choose. These mechanisms are the impersonal forces of the market, and if they are in any way coercive, it is simply in the sense that they compel economic actors to act "rationally" so as to maximize choice and opportunity. This implies that capitalism, the ultimate "market society," is the optimal condition of opportunity and choice. More goods and services are on offer, more people are more free to sell and profit from them, and more people are more free to choose among and buy them.

So what is wrong with this conception? A socialist is likely to say that the major missing ingredient is the commodification of labor power and class exploitation. So far so good. But what may not always be so clear, even in socialist accounts of the market, is that the distinctive and dominant characteristic of the capitalist market is not opportunity or choice but, on the contrary, compulsion. This is so in two senses: first, that material life and social reproduction in capitalism are universally mediated by the market, so that all individuals must in one way or another enter into market relations in order to gain access to the means of life; and second, that the dictates of the capitalist market—its imperatives of competition, accumulation, profit maximization, and increasing labor productivity—regulate not only all economic transactions but social relations in general. As relations among human beings are mediated by the process of commodity exchange, social relations among people appear as relations among things, the "fetishism of commodities," in Marx's famous phrase.

Some readers are likely to object here that this is something every socialist, or at least every Marxist, knows. But the specificities of capitalism, like the operation of the capitalist market as imperative rather than opportunity, tend to get lost even in Marxist histories of capitalism. The capitalist market as a specific social form gets lost when the transition from pre-capitalist to capitalist societies is presented as a more or less natural, if often thwarted, extension or maturation of already existing social forms, more a quantitative than a qualitative transformation.

This little book is about the origin of capitalism and about the controversies it has evoked, both historical and theoretical. Part One is a survey of the most important historical accounts and the debates surrounding them. It will deal in particular with the most common model of capitalist development, the so-called commercialization model, in several of its variants, and also with some of the main challenges to it. Part Two sketches an alternative history which, I hope, avoids some of the most common pitfalls of the standard question-begging explanations. This sketch is deeply indebted to those histories of capitalism, discussed in Part One, that have questioned some of the prevailing historical conventions. My intention is above all to challenge the naturalization of capitalism and to highlight the particular ways in which it represents a historically specific social form and a rupture with earlier social forms.

The purpose of this exercise is both scholarly and political. The naturalization of capitalism, which denies its specificity and the long and painful historical processes that brought it into being, limits our understanding of the past. At the same time, it restricts our hopes and expectations for the future, for if capitalism is the natural culmination of history, then surmounting it is unimaginable. The question of the origin of capitalism may seem arcane, but it goes to the heart of assumptions deeply rooted in our culture, widespread and dangerous illusions about the so-called free market and its benefits to humanity. Thinking about future alternatives to capitalism requires us to explore alternative conceptions of its past.

Part One

Histories of the Transition

Chapter One

The Commercialization Model and Its Legacy

THE MOST COMMON WAY OF EXPLAINING THE ORIGIN OF capitalism is to presuppose that its development is the natural outcome of human practices almost as old as the species itself, which required only the removal of external obstacles that hindered its realization. This mode of explanation, or non-explanation, although it has existed in many variants, constitutes what has been called the "commercialization model" of economic development, and this model is arguably still the dominant one. This is so even among its harshest critics. It is not entirely absent from the demographic explanations that claim to have displaced it, or even from most Marxist accounts.

The Commercialization Model

Far from recognizing that the market became capitalist when it became compulsory, most historical accounts suggest that capitalism emerged when the market was liberated from age-old constraints and when, for one reason or another, opportunities for trade expanded. In these accounts, capitalism represents not so much a qualitative break from earlier forms as a massive quantitative increase: an expansion of markets and a growing commercialization of economic life.

The traditional account—which appears in classical political economy, Enlightenment conceptions of progress, and many more modern histories—is as follows. With or without a natural inclination to "truck, barter, and exchange" (in Adam Smith's famous formulation), rationally self-interested individuals have been engaging in acts of exchange since the dawn of history. These acts became increasingly specialized with an evolving division of labor, which was also accompanied by technical improvements in the instruments of production. Improvements in productivity, in many of these explanations, may in fact have been the primary purpose of the increasingly specialized division of labor, so that there tends to be a close connection between these accounts of commercial development and a kind of technological determinism. Capitalism, then, or "commercial society," the highest stage of progress, represents a maturation of age-old commercial practices (together with technical advances) and their liberation from political and cultural constraints.

But only in the West, the story goes, were these constraints comprehensively and decisively lifted. In the ancient Mediterranean, commercial society was already fairly well established, but its further evolution was interrupted by an unnatural break—the hiatus of feudalism, and several dark centuries during which economic life was again fettered by irrationalism and the political parasitism of landlordly power.

The classical explanation of this interruption invokes barbarian invasions of the Roman Empire, but a later and very influential version of this model was elaborated by the Belgian historian Henri Pirenne. Pirenne situated the rupture of the Mediterranean commercial civilization rather later, in the Muslim invasion, which, he argued, suppressed the old commercial system by closing off the Mediterranean trade routes between East and West. A growing "economy of exchange," led by a professional class of merchants, was replaced by an "economy of consumption," the rentier economy of the feudal aristocracy.[1]

But eventually, according to both Pirenne and his predecessors, commerce revived with the growth of cities and the liberation of merchants. Here we come to one of the most common assumptions associated with the commercialization model, the association of capitalism with cities—indeed, the assumption that cities are from the beginning capitalism in embryo. In Europe, the argument goes, cities emerged with distinctive and unprecedented autonomy, cities devoted to trade and dominated by an autonomous burgher (or bourgeois) class which was to free itself once and for all from the fetters of the old cultural constraints and political parasitism. This liberation of the urban economy, of commercial activity and mercantile rationality, accompanied by the inevitable improvements in techniques of production which evidently follow from the emancipation of trade, was apparently enough to account for the rise of modern capitalism.

All these explanations have in common certain assumptions about the continuity of trade and markets, from their earliest manifestations in exchange to their maturity in modern industrial capitalism. The age-old practice of commercial profit-taking in the form of "buying cheap and selling dear" is not, in these accounts, fundamentally different from capitalist exchange and accumulation through the appropriation of surplus value.

There also tends to be another common theme in these histories of capitalism: the bourgeois as agent of progress. We have become so used to the identification of *bourgeois* with *capitalist* that the presuppositions secreted in this conflation have become invisible to us. The burgher or bourgeois is, by definition, a town-dweller. Beyond that, specifically in its French form, the word used to mean nothing more than someone of non-noble status who, while he worked for a living, did not generally dirty his hands and used his mind more than his body in his work. That old usage tells us nothing about capitalism, and is likely to refer to a professional, an office-holder, or an intellectual no less than to a merchant. In the slippage from town-dweller to capitalist via the merchant which occurs in the later uses of "bourgeois," we can follow the logic of the commercialization model: the ancient town-dweller gives way to the medieval burgher, who in turn develops seamlessly into the modern capitalist. As a famous historian has sardonically described this process, history is the perennial rise of the middle classes.

This is not to say that all historians who subscribe to such models have failed to acknowledge that capitalism represents a historical break or transformation of one kind or another. It is true that some have tended to find not just trade but a bit of capitalism itself almost everywhere, especially in Greek and Roman antiquity, always just waiting to be released from extraneous impediments. But even they have generally insisted on a major shift from the economic principles of feudalism to the new rationality of "commercial society," or capitalism. People have often talked, for example, about the transition from a "natural" economy to a money economy, or even from production for use to production for exchange. Yet if there is a major transformation in these historical accounts, it is not in the nature of trade and markets themselves. The change is rather in what happens to the forces and institutions—political, legal, cultural, and ideological, as well as technological—that have impeded the natural evolution of trade and the maturation of markets.

If anything, in these models it is *feudalism* that represents the real historic rupture. The resumption of commercial development, beginning in the interstices of feudalism and then breaking through its constraints, is treated as a major change in the history of Europe, but it appears as a resumption of a historical process that was temporarily—if drastically and for a rather long time—deflected. These assumptions tend to have another important corollary, namely that towns and trade were by nature antithetical to feudalism, so that their growth, however it came about, undermined the foundations of the feudal system.

But if feudalism had derailed the progress of commercial society, the intrinsic logic of the market, according to these explanations, never significantly changed. From the beginning, it involved rationally self-interested individuals maximizing their utilities by selling goods for profit whenever the opportunity presented itself. More particularly, it involved an increasing division of labor and specialization, requiring ever more elaborate networks of trade, and, above all, ever-improving productive techniques to cut costs and enhance commercial profits. This logic could in various ways be thwarted. It could even be more or less completely submerged—so that, for example, feudal lords could suppress it, appropriating not by engaging in profitable exchange or encouraging the improvement of productive techniques but rather by exploiting forced labor, squeezing surplus labor out of peasants by means of superior power. But in principle, the logic of the market remained ever the same: always an opportunity to be taken whenever possible, always conducive to economic growth and the improvement of productive forces, always bound eventually to produce industrial capitalism, if left free to work out its natural logic.

In other words, the commercialization model made no acknowledgement of imperatives specific to capitalism, of the specific ways in which the market operates in capitalism, of its specific laws of motion which uniquely compel people to enter the market and compel producers to produce "efficiently" by improving labor productivity—the laws of competition, profit maximization, and capital accumulation. It follows that adherents of this model saw no need to explain the specific social property relations and the specific mode of exploitation that determine these specific laws of motion.

There was, in fact, no need in the commercialization model to explain the emergence of capitalism at all. It assumed that capitalism had existed, at least in embryo, from the dawn of history, if not in the very core of human nature and human rationality. People, it assumed, given the chance, have always behaved according to the rules of capitalist rationality, pursuing profit and in its pursuit seeking ways to improve labor productivity. So history in effect had proceeded by the laws of capitalist development, in a process of economic growth sustained by developing productive forces, albeit with some major interruptions. If the emergence of a mature capitalist economy required any explanation, it was to identify the barriers that have stood in the way of its natural development, and the process by which those barriers were lifted.

There is, of course, a major paradox here. The market was supposed to be an arena of choice, and "commercial society" the perfection of freedom. Yet this conception of the market seems to rule out human freedom. It has tended to be associated with a theory of history in which modern capitalism is the outcome of an almost natural and inevitable process, following certain universal, transhistorical, and immutable laws. The operation of these laws can, at least temporarily, be thwarted, but not without great cost. And its end product, the "free" market, is an impersonal mechanism which can to some extent be controlled and regulated, but which cannot finally be thwarted without all the dangers— and the futility—entailed by any attempt to violate the laws of nature.

After the Classic Commercialization Model

There have been various refinements of the basic commercialization model, from Max Weber to Fernand Braudel.[2] Weber certainly did not fail to see that a fully developed capitalism emerged only in very specific historical conditions and not in others. He was more than willing to see some kind of capitalism in earlier times, even in classical antiquity. But he did, after all, set out to distinguish Europe from other parts of the world, and he did, of course, emphasize the uniqueness of the Western city and European religion, especially in order to explain the unique development of Western capitalism. The point, however, is that he always tended to talk about the factors that *impeded* the development of capitalism in other places—their kinship forms, their forms of domination, their religious traditions, and so on—as if the natural, *un*-impeded growth of towns and trade and the liberation of towns and burgher classes would by definition mean capitalism. Weber also, it should be added, shares with many others the assumption that the development of capitalism was a trans-European (or Western European) process—not only that certain general European circumstances were necessary conditions for capitalism but that all of Europe, for all its internal variations, followed essentially one historical path.

More recently, there have been frontal attacks on the commercialization model in general and the Pirenne thesis in particular, which is now generally out of favor. Among the most recent and influential of these has been the demographic model, which attributes European economic development to certain autonomous cycles of population growth and decline. But however vehemently the old model has been challenged, it is not really clear that the fundamental presuppositions of the demographic explanation are as far removed from the commercialization model as its exponents claim.

The underlying premise of the demographic model is, after all, that the transition to capitalism was determined by the laws of supply and demand.[3] Those laws might be determined in more complicated ways than the commercialization model could account for. They might have less to do with the social processes of urbanization and growing trade than with complex cyclical patterns of population growth and decline, or Malthusian blockages. But the transition to capitalism is still a response to the universal and transhistorical laws of the market, the laws of supply and demand. The nature of the market and its laws is never really questioned.

The demographic model certainly challenges conventional arguments about the primacy of expanding trade as a determinant in European economic development. It may not even deny, at least explicitly, that the capitalist market is qualititively different from, and not just quantitatively larger and more inclusive than, markets in non-capitalist societies. But neither does it represent a frontal challenge to that convention, and in effect takes it for granted.

In a variation on the old commercialization theme, some historians have suggested that capitalism was the result of an incremental process in which, as the center of commercial gravity shifted from one European locale to another—from the Italian city-states to the Netherlands or the cities of the Hanse, and from Spanish colonial expansion to other imperialisms, culminating in the British Empire—each built upon the accomplishments of the last, not only expanding the reach of European trade but also refining its instruments, from the techniques of double-entry bookkeeping in Italy to improvements in productive technologies, culminating in the English industrial revolution. The end result of this "value-added process" (perhaps with the help of bourgeois revolutions) was modern capitalism.[4]

In one way or another, then, whether by processes of urbanization and growing trade or by the cyclical patterns of demographic growth, the transition to capitalism in all these explanations is a response to the universal and transhistorical laws of the market. Needless to say, neo-classical economics has done nothing to displace these assumptions—not least because it is generally uninterested in history altogether. As for historians today, those interested in the *longue durée* are likely to belong to the demographic school, unless they are more interested in *mentalités* or discourse than in economic processes. Others, especially in the English-speaking world, are generally suspicious of long-term processes altogether and are more interested in very local or episodic histories and in proximate causes. They do not actually *challenge* the existing theories of long-term development so much as they merely dismiss or evade them.[5]

The new wave of historical sociology is different. It is, of course, primarily interested in long-term processes of social change. But even here there is a tendency to beg the question in various ways. For instance, in one of the most important recent works in this genre, Michael Mann explicitly adopts what he calls a "teleological bias," according to which industrial capitalism is already prefigured in medieval European social arrangements.[6] Not surprisingly, for all its complexities his argument situates the driving force of European development in the "acceleration of intensive powers of economic praxis" and the "extensive growth of commodity circuits"—in other words, technological progress and commercial expansion.[7] And this explanation depends, yet again, on the absence of constraints: capitalism was free to develop in Europe because an essentially "acephalous" social organization (the decentralized, fragmented political order of feudalism) left various actors (notably merchants) a substantial degree of autonomy (with the help of the "rationalism" and normative order provided by Christianity). Furthermore, private property was allowed to develop into *capitalist* property because no community or class organization possessed monopoly powers. In short, not only the emergence of capitalism but its eventual and apparently inevitable maturation into its industrial form are explained above all by a series of *absences*. If only by default, then, the traditional "commercialization model" still prevails, whether on the surface or in more subterranean form.

A Notable Exception: Karl Polanyi

In his classic, *The Great Transformation* (1944), and other works, the economic historian and anthropologist Karl Polanyi maintained that the motive of individual profit associated with market exchange was never till the modern age the dominant principle of economic life.[8] Even where markets were well-developed, a sharp distinction must be made, he said, between societies with markets, such as have existed throughout recorded history, and a "market society." In all earlier societies, "economic" relations and practices were "embedded" or submerged in non-economic— kinship, communal, religious, and political—relationships. There have been other motives driving economic activity than the purely "economic" motives of profit and material gain, such as the achievement of status and prestige, or the maintenance of communal solidarity. There have been other ways of organizing economic life than through the mechanisms of market exchange, in particular "reciprocity" and "redistribution"—elaborate reciprocal obligations determined, for instance, by kinship, or the authoritative appropriation of surpluses by some kind of political or religious power and their redistribution from that center.

Polanyi directly challenged Adam Smith's assumptions about "economic man" and his natural "propensity to truck, barter, and exchange," arguing that this "propensity" had never before Smith's own time played the dominant role he assigned to it, and that it did not *regulate* the economy until a century later. Where markets did exist in pre-market societies, even where they were extensive and important, they remained a subordinate feature of economic life, dominated by other principles of economic behavior. Not only that, these markets, even in the most wide-ranging and complex commercial systems, operated according to a logic quite distinct from that of the modern capitalist market.

In particular, neither the local markets nor the long-distance trade characteristic of pre-capitalist economies were essentially competitive (let alone, he might have added, *driven* by competition). These forms of trade—between town and country in the one case and climatic zones in the other—were, he suggests, more "complementary" than competitive (even, evidently, when "complementarity" was distorted by unequal power relations). External trade was simply "carrying." Here, the merchant's job was to move goods from one market to another, while in local trade, he argued, commercial activity was strictly regulated and exclusive. In general, competition was deliberately eliminated because it tended to disorganize trade.

Polanyi points out that only internal, national markets—a very late development, much resisted by local merchants and autonomous towns in the most advanced commercial centers of Europe—were to be conducted according to competitive principles. But even internal markets within early modern European nation-states were for some time simply a loose collection of separate municipal markets, joined by a carrying trade hardly different in principle from long-distance, overseas commerce. Nor was an integrated internal market a direct descendant of, or a natural evolution from, the local or long-distance trade which preceded it. It was, Polanyi argues, a product of state intervention—and even then, in an economy still largely based on production by self-sufficient peasant households laboring for subsistence, state regulation continued to prevail over competitive principles.

Only in modern "market society," according to Polanyi, is there a distinct "economic" motive, distinct economic institutions and relations separated from non-economic relations. Because human beings and nature—in the form of labor and land—are treated, however fictitiously, as commodities in a self-regulating system of markets driven by the price mechanism, society itself becomes an "adjunct" of the market. A market *economy* can exist only in a market *society,* that is, a society where, instead of an economy embedded in social relations, social relations are embedded in society.

Polanyi was not, of course, alone in noting the secondary role of the market in pre-capitalist societies. Any competent economic historian or anthropologist is bound to acknowledge the various non-market principles of economic behavior that operated in such societies, from the most "primitive" and egalitarian to the most elaborate, stratified, and exploitative "high" civilizations. And other economic historians (though perhaps not as many as one might imagine) have taken note of certain changes in the principles of trade. But Polanyi's account is particularly notable for its stark delineation of the rupture between "market society" and the non-market societies which preceded it, even societies with markets—not only the differences between their economic logics but the social dislocations which that transformation brought about. So disruptive was the system of self-regulating markets, Polanyi insists, not only to social relations but to the human psyche, so awful its effects on human lives, that the history of its implantation had to be at the same time the history of protection from its ravages. Without "protective countermoves," particularly by means of state intervention, "human society would have been annihilated."[9]

This argument in many ways represents a dramatic departure from accounts of economic development that stress the (more or less benign) continuities between ancient commerce and the modern capitalist economy, even when they observe the antagonism between "commercial" or capitalist principles and the economic (or anti-economic) logic of feudalism. But in some important respects, Polanyi's account retains significant affinities with more conventional economic histories. The main problems have to do with Polanyi's explanation of the conditions in which market society emerged, the historical process that brought it into being, and what this implies about his understanding of the market as a social form. This is not the place to enter into a detailed debate about the nature of medieval English land tenure, "mercantilism," the Speenhamland system, or other specific historical questions about which specialists today would have reason to take issue with Polanyi. The issue here is the broader sweep of Polanyi's historical narrative and its consequences for our understanding of modern capitalism.

There is, first, more than a little technological determinism in his argument. The main theme of Polanyi's historical account is how the Industrial Revolution brought about a market society—how, in a commercial society, the invention of complex machines made it necessary to convert "the natural and human substance of society into commodities."[10] "Since elaborate machines are expensive, they do not pay unless large amounts of goods are produced," he wrote, and to achieve the necessary scale of production, the production must be uninterrupted, which means that, for the merchant, "all factors involved must be on sale."[11] The ultimate and most disastrous step in creating the necessary conditions—that is, in creating the market society originally required by complex machine production—is the transformation of labor into a commodified "factor."

The sequence of causation here is significant. The Industrial Revolution was "merely the beginning" of an "extreme and radical" revolution which utterly transformed society by commodifying humanity and nature.[12] That transformation, then, was the effort of technological progress. At its heart was "an almost miraculous improvement in the tools of production";[13] and, while it brought about a transformation of society, it was itself the culmination of earlier improvements in productivity, both in techniques and in the organization of land use, notably enclosures in England.

Although Polanyi takes issue with the belief in "spontaneous progress," he never for a moment seems to doubt the inevitability of such improvements, at least in the context of Western commercial society, with its "free institutions," especially its free urban communes, and the expansion of trade—what he calls "the Western European trend of economic progress."[14] His argument against conventional views of spontaneous progress is simply that they fail to consider the role of the state in affecting—and, more particularly, slowing down—the rate of change (as the Tudor and early Stuart state slowed down enclosure). Without such interventions, "the rate of that progress might have been ruinous, and have turned the process itself into a degenerative instead of a constructive event," just as the Industrial Revolution itself required state intervention to preserve the social fabric.[15]

The main outlines of Polanyi's historical narrative, then, are in some respects not entirely different from the old commercialization model: the expansion of markets goes hand in hand with technological progress to produce modern industrial capitalism. And although the process culminates in England, it is a general European process. For that matter, it appears that the process which led from commercialization to industrialization to "market society" may after all have been a more or less natural development in an increasingly commercialized world, a development completed only in Europe simply because certain non-economic obstacles did not here block its path. As a student of Polanyi's has explained in an account of Polanyi's lectures on "General Economic History," Polanyi argued that, in contrast to an equally commercialized East, Western European feudalism was not characterized by strong bonds of kinship, clan, and tribe, so that "when feudal ties weakened and disappeared, there was little to stand in the way of domination by market forces." And while government intervention was required to create "factor markets," "the developing market economy helped to destroy feudal economic and political institutions."[16]

What fails to emerge from all of this is an appreciation of the ways in which a radical transformation of social relations *preceded* industrialization. The revolutionizing of productive forces *presupposed* a transformation of property relations and a change in the form of exploitation that created a historically unique *need* to improve the productivity of labor. It *presupposed* the emergence of capitalist imperatives: competition, accumulation, and profit maximization. To say this is not just to accuse Polanyi of putting the cart before the horse. The more fundamental point is that his order of causation suggests a failure to treat the capitalist market itself as a specific social form. The specific imperatives of the capitalist market—the pressures of accumulation and increasing labor productivity—are treated not as the product of specific social relations but as a result of technological improvements that seem more or less inevitable, at least in Europe.

The fact remains that *The Great Transformation* was a significant departure from conventional historiography on the "transition." Yet it is striking how little that important book has managed to affect the dominant model, even though there now seems to be a revival of interest in Polanyi. In general, we are still where we were. Either the question of capitalism and its origins does not arise at all, or else, even when questions are raised about how and why capitalism *did* emerge in some special case or cases, they tend to be overtaken by another question: why did capitalism *not* emerge in others? Some readers may, for example, be familiar with the idea of "failed transitions" as a way of describing what happened—or failed to happen—in the commerical city-states of northern Italy, or in the Netherlands. That phrase, "failed transition," says it all.

How we understand capitalism's history has a lot to do with how we understand the thing itself. The old models of capitalist development were a paradoxical blend of transhistorical determinism and "free" market voluntarism, in which the capitalist market was both an immutable natural law and the perfection of human choice and freedom. The antithesis of such models would be a conception of the capitalist market that fully acknowledges its imperatives and compulsions, while recognizing that these imperatives themselves are rooted not in some transhistorical natural law but in historically specific social relations, constituted by human agency and subject to change. This is the kind of conception we might expect to find in Marxism, but Marxist historians have not consistently provided that kind of alternative.

Chapter Two

Marxist Debates

IN THESE HISTORICAL DEBATES, THERE HAS BEEN AS MUCH disagreement among Marxists as between Marxist and non-Marxist historians. Many Marxists have been no less wedded than anyone else to the old commercialization model, often, perhaps, with an even stronger dose of technological determinism. Others have been very critical of that model, though even here some residues remain. With the debate still in progress, there is still much work to be done.

Matters are not helped by the fact that there are two different narratives in Marx's own work.[1] One is very much like the conventional model, where history is a succession of stages in the division of labor, with a transhistorical process of technological progress, and the leading role assigned to burgher classes who seem to bring about capitalism just by being liberated from feudal chains. In fact, capitalism already exists in feudalism, in a way, in the "interstices of feudalism," to use Marx's words, and it enters the mainstream of history when it "bursts asunder" the fetters of feudalism. This is basically the narrative of such earlier writings as *The German Ideology* and *The Communist Manifesto*. And this is the narrative at least implicit in traditional Marxist ideas of "bourgeois revolution." But there is another story, or at least the foundations of one, in the *Grundrisse* and *Capital*, which has more to do with changing property relations, especially in the English countryside: the expropriation of direct producers that gave rise to a new form of exploitation and new systemic "laws of motion." The most important Marxist histories since then have built upon those foundations.

The Transition Debate

Instead of exploring Marx's own ideas in detail, let us look at more recent Marxist histories. We can leave out of account altogether the crudest kinds of technological determinism which have all too often passed as Marxist theories of history, concentrating instead on the most serious and challenging Marxist accounts.

In 1950, a exchange took place between the economist Paul Sweezy and the economic historian Maurice Dobb, whose *Studies in the Development of Capitalism* (1946) Sweezy had criticized. Their exchange expanded into a major debate among a wide range of distinguished, mainly Marxist, historians in the journal *Science & Society* that was later collected and published as a book.[2] The debate came to be known as the "transition debate," and it has been a central reference point for discussion of the subject among Marxists—and others—ever since.

Dobb's work represented a major advance in understanding the transition. It represented a powerful challenge to the old commercialization model in so far as it situated the origins of capitalism in the countryside, in the primary feudal relations between landlords and peasants. Like other work in this tradition, most notably the writings of the historian of medieval Europe, R. H. Hilton, this analysis undermined the foundations of the old model, calling into question some of its basic premises, especially the assumption that the antithesis to feudalism, which dissolved it and gave rise to capitalism, was to be found in towns and in trade.

The central question at issue between Sweezy and Dobb was where to locate the "prime mover" in the transition from feudalism to capitalism. Was the primary cause of the transition to be found within the basic, constitutive relations of feudalism, the relations between lords and peasants? Or was the prime mover external to those relations, located particularly in the expansion of trade?

Dobb and, in the ensuing debate, Hilton made profoundly important arguments demonstrating that trade was not in itself the solvent of feudalism. In fact, trade and towns were not inherently inimical to feudalism at all. Instead, feudalism was dissolved and capitalism brought about by factors internal to the primary relations of feudalism itself, in the class struggles between lords and peasants. Hilton in particular pointed out that Pirenne's argument had been shown to be empirically flawed, and he spelled out the ways in which money, trade, towns and even the so-called "commercial revolution" were not alien, but on the contrary, integral to the feudal system. This meant that while there was undoubtedly a complex process in which these factors contributed to the transition, they could not be regarded as the solvent of feudalism.

Both Dobb and Hilton in various ways suggested that the dissolution of feudalism and the rise of capitalism resulted from the *liberation* of petty commodity production, its release from the fetters of feudalism, largely by means of class struggle between lords and peasants. Dobb, for example, argued that, while class struggle did not, "in any simple and direct way," give rise to capitalism, it did serve to "modify the dependence of the petty mode of production upon feudal overlordship and eventually to shake loose the small producer from feudal exploitation. It is then from the petty mode of production (in the degree to which it secures independence of action, and social differentiation in turn develops within it) that capitalism is born."[3]

Similarly, Hilton, whose studies on medieval peasants and their struggles represent some of the most important work in the historiography of *any* period, traced the transition to struggles between lords and peasants. The pressures imposed by lords on peasants to transfer surplus labor was, he suggested, the root cause of improved production techniques and the basis for the growth of simple commodity production. At the same time, peasant resistance to those pressures was crucially important to the process of transition to capitalism, "the freeing of peasant and artisan economies for the development of commodity production and eventually the emergence of the capitalist entrepreneur."[4]

Sweezy, in his counter-argument, insisted that feudalism, for all its inefficiencies and instabilities, was intrinsically tenacious and resistant to change, and that the main moving force in its dissolution had to come from outside. The feudal system could tolerate, and indeed required, a certain amount of trade; but with the establishment of localized urban trading and trans-shipment centers based on long-distance trade (about which Sweezy cited the authority of Henri Pirenne), a process was set in train that encouraged the growth of production for exchange, in tension with the feudal principle of production for use.

Nevertheless, capitalism was not, Sweezy argued, the immediate outcome of this process. The expansion of trade was sufficient to dissolve feudalism, and to usher in a transitional phase of "pre-capitalist commodity production" which was itself unstable, preparing the ground for capitalism in the seventeenth and eighteenth centuries; but there was a subsequent distinct phase in the development of capitalism. Sweezy here made the important point that, "We usually think of a transition from one social system to another as a process in which the two systems directly confront each other and fight it out for supremacy," but it would be a "serious error" to think of the transition from feudalism to capitalism in these terms.[5]

Sweezy did not propose to explain the second phase of the process, but he raised some critical questions about explanations offered by others. Two in particular stand out. First, he expressed skepticism about the plausibility of the view—following from the conventional interpretation of Marx's theory of the "really revolutionary way" to industrial capitalism—that industrial capitalists rose from the ranks of petty producers. He proposed instead that we should understand the "really revolutionary way" as a process in which the producer, instead of growing from petty producer into merchant and capitalist, *"starts out* as both a merchant and an employer of wage-labor," in which capitalist enterprises are launched fully fledged instead of in a gradual process emerging out of the putting-out system.[6]

Sweezy's second point was that the generalization of commodity production could not account for the rise of capitalism, and that highly developed commodity production—as, for instance, in medieval Italy or Flanders—did not necessarily produce capitalism.[7] In the course of his argument, he made another suggestive point. In opposition to Maurice Dobb's theory that the decline of feudalism resulted from the over-exploitation of peasants and the class conflicts engendered by it, Sweezy proposed that it might be "more accurate to say that the decline of western European feudalism was due to the inability of the ruling class to maintain control over, and hence to exploit, society's labor power."[8]

This summary is, of course, a gross abbreviation and simplification of the complex arguments offered by the participants in the debate, but it should be enough to raise some critical questions about the assumptions on which each side was operating. At first glance, the issue seems pretty clear: Dobb was attacking the commercialization model, while Sweezy was defending it. In fact, some time later the Marxist historian Robert Brenner accused

Sweezy, together with others such as Andre Gunder Frank and Immanuel Wallerstein, of being "neo-Smithian" precisely because of their adherence to something like the classic commercialization model as outlined first by Adam Smith.[9] Brenner made a powerful argument about the way some Marxists have effectively swallowed the assumptions of the old model, the tendency to treat the specific dynamic of capitalism—and its need for increasing labor productivity—as an inevitable outcome of commercial expansion. But there was something more complex going on in the debate between Sweezy and Dobb.

On the face of it, Sweezy's argument is, in its main outlines, completely consistent with the commercialization model, while Dobb's account is a frontal attack on it. To the extent that Sweezy proceeds from the Pirenne thesis in particular, and more generally suggests a fundamental antagonism between the growing system of long-distance trade and the basic principles of feudalism, or sometimes ascribes to pre-capitalist economic actors a rationality specific to capitalism, it will by now be clear to readers that the argument of this book differs from his. The argument laid out here, especially in Part Two, is consistent with, indeed influenced by, Dobb and Hilton on several major points: that towns and trade were not by nature necessarily inimical to feudalism, that the "prime mover" is to be found within the primary property relations of feudalism, and that class struggle between lords and peasants was central to the process.

But there was more to the debate than that. Sweezy made one point that tends to get lost in considerations of the transition debate. He certainly did ascribe the dissolution of feudalism to the effects of commercial expansion and the growth of towns. But Sweezy insisted that the dissolution of feudalism was not enough to account for the rise of capitalism, that these were actually two distinct processes. Here we find an interesting contrast between Sweezy and Dobb: Dobb seems *more* inclined than Sweezy to treat the dissolution of feudalism as essentially the same process as the rise of capitalism.

Why is this significant? Consider the implications of such an argument: if the dissolution of feudalism is sufficient to explain the rise of capitalism, are we not very close again to the assumptions of the commercialization model? We may now be in the countryside instead of in the town, and we may be focusing on class struggle between lords and peasants instead of on the expansion of trade. But one critical assumption stays the same: capitalism emerges when the fetters of feudalism are removed. Capitalism is somehow already present in the interstices of feudalism, just waiting there to be released.

Dobb and Hilton thus do not seem to be challenging all the basic assumptions of the commercialization model, and some of the questions raised by Sweezy go to the heart of the problems they leave unresolved. One point stands out in the arguments of Dobb and Hilton: the transition to capitalism is a matter of liberating or "shaking loose" an economic logic already present in simple commodity production. We are left with the overwhelming impression that, given the chance, the commodity-producing peasant (and artisan) will grow into a capitalist. The center of gravity in this argument has shifted away from the city to the countryside, and class struggle has been given a new role, but how different are the assumptions underlying this argument from some of the the main premises of the commercialization model? How far are we from the premise that the capitalist market is an opportunity rather than an imperative, and that what requires explanation in accounting for the rise of capitalism is the removal of obstacles, the breaking of fetters, and not the creation of a wholly new economic logic? Class struggle is central to the process, but above all as a means of removing obstacles to something that was already immanent.

Here the problems that troubled Sweezy in his confrontation with Dobb's argument are very much to the point. First, the habit of treating transitions as a confrontation between two antithetical modes of production has far too often been an excuse for begging the question. As Sweezy suggested, while that assumption may apply to the transition from capitalism to socialism, it is problematic in dealing with the transition from feudalism to capitalism. As we have seen, the commercialization model and other related explanations effectively assume the existence of capitalism, or a capitalist rationality, in order to explain its emergence. Feudalism is confronted by an already existing capitalism, or at least an already existing capitalist logic of process, whose coming into being is never explained. The explanations offered by Marxists like Hilton and Dobb, while in many ways devastating to the commercialization model and to its assumptions about the antithesis of feudalism and commerce, have not entirely escaped this trap, for they still in some important respects assume the very thing that needs to be explained.

Nor do they offer an entirely convincing response to the question raised by Sweezy about the "failure" of advanced commercial centers such as those of Italy and Flanders. Here again there is a tendency to take capitalism for granted by simply explaining the *obstacles* that prevented these commercial cities from reaching maturity. The question posed about Flanders or Italy is not so much why and in what circumstances did capitalist imperatives impose themselves on economic actors, as they did in England, but rather why and in what ways were economic actors in the "failed" transitions unwilling or unable—not least for ideological or cultural reasons—to break away from their attachment to feudalism in order to create a new social form?[10]

As for Sweezy's doubts about the "really revolutionary way," later in the debate he did withdraw some of his objections to the conventional interpretation of what Marx had in mind but not necessarily his objections to the idea itself. While he never fully explained the reasons for his unease about the idea that capitalism emerged as petty commodity producers transformed themselves into capitalists, he seemed to find it inherently implausible. And there were indeed good grounds for his skepticism.

Although Sweezy was primarily interested here in the rise of industrial capitalism, the "really revolutionary way" appears in Dobb more particularly (though not exclusively) in the form of capitalist farmers rising from the ranks of the yeomanry. The problem is not that these rising yeomen are given credit for creating capitalism but more particularly that they tend to be depicted as more or less freely choosing the capitalist road, once released from feudal impediments, while capitalism is treated as a more or less organic growth out of petty commodity production—even if bourgeois revolutions may be required to remove the final obstacles. Whatever Sweezy may have had in mind in his objection to the "really revolutionary way," it would certainly be reasonable to say that something more is required to account for the disposition of producers to behave like capitalists than simply their liberation from restraints or their growth from "middling" to large proprietors. In other words, there is a qualitative, not simply a quantitative, difference between petty commodity production and capitalism, a difference that remains to be explained.

Perry Anderson on Absolutism and Capitalism

In the 1970s, when he was editor of *New Left Review,* another influential Marxist, Perry Anderson, published two magisterial volumes of what was intended to be a trilogy, beginning with a study of the transition from Graeco-Roman antiquity to European feudalism (*Passages from Antiquity to Feudalism*), continuing with an analysis of European absolutism (*Lineages of the Absolutist State*), and culminating in a study of bourgeois revolutions and the development of capitalism. Although that third volume, which was to complete his account of the transition to capitalism, has not yet appeared, there is much to be learned from the first two, especially *Lineages,* and from various bits and pieces elsewhere.

For our purposes, we can begin with Anderson's definition of feudalism as a mode of production defined by "an organic *unity* of economy and polity," which took the form of a "chain of parcellized sovereignties," together with a hierarchical chain of conditional property. State power was fragmented among feudal lords, and lordship represented a unity of political and economic power. The fragment of state power that feudal lords possessed—their political, juridical, and military powers—at one and the same time constituted their economic power to appropriate surplus labor from dependent peasants. Lordship was accompanied by "a mechanism of surplus extraction," serfdom, in which "economic exploitation and politico-legal coercion were fused."[11]

But something happened that made this feudal formation unstable. The old feudal bonds were weakened by the commutation of feudal dues into money rents, and, more particularly, by the growth of a commodity economy. "With the generalised commutation of dues into money rents," Anderson argues, "the cellular unity of political and economic oppression of the peasantry was gravely weakened, and threatened to become dissociated. The result was a *displacement* of politico-legal coercion upwards towards a centralized, militarized summit—the Absolutist State."[12] In other words, in order to strengthen their weakened hold on the peasantry, feudal lords concentrated their formerly fragmented or parcellized coercive powers in a new kind of centralized monarchy.

Meanwhile, in the interstices of the fragmented feudal system, in the town, an economic sphere had emerged that was not controlled by the aristocracy. At the same time, these towns became the site of technical innovations. Anderson concludes that, while "the political order remained feudal . . . society became more and more bourgeois."[13]

The emergence of absolutism represents a critical step in Anderson's argument about the rise of capitalism. Absolutism itself was not a capitalist or proto-capitalist state. It was, if anything, essentially feudal in its basic structure, *"a redeployed and recharged apparatus of feudal domination,* designed to clamp the peasant masses back into their traditional social position."[14] But it was a pivotal moment in the development of capitalism.

Ironically, the effect of this displacement upwards of feudal coercive power—at least its principal contribution to the evolution of capitalism, according to Anderson—was to *fracture* the unity of economy and polity which had characterized feudalism. On the one hand, political power was concentrated in the royal state. On the other hand, the economy began to achieve a certain autonomy. As politico-legal coercion was "displaced upwards," the commodity economy and the "bourgeois society" which had grown in the interstices of feudalism were liberated and allowed to develop on their own terms.

That, then, is Anderson's conception of absolutism in broad outline. And much of it is very illuminating, too. His characterization of the absolutist state as essentially feudal is especially useful, though it demands closer scrutiny. Keep in mind what Anderson means. The absolutist state was essentially feudal, he insists, because it represented the displacement upward and the centralization of the feudal lords' politico-legal coercive powers, separating those powers from economic exploitation. To put it another way, the absolutist state separated the two moments of exploitation, the process of surplus extraction on the one hand and the coercive power that sustains it on the other. The two then continued in separate spheres. The feudal fusion of economy and polity started giving way to the separation characteristic of capitalism, leaving the "economy" to evolve according to its own internal logic.

Now, there is another way of looking at absolutism, which is that it represents a centralization of feudal power in a different sense: namely that the monarchical state itself becomes a form of property, an instrument of appropriation, in ways analogous to feudal lordship. Economic and political power are still fused, but the lord appropriates rents while the state and its officeholders appropriate peasant surpluses in the form of tax. Sometimes Anderson does seem to think of absolutism in these terms, as still a unity of economic and political spheres. But his whole argument that absolutism plays a pivotal role in the transition to capitalism depends on the essential function of the absolutist state in *separating* political and economic spheres. He is at great pains to emphasize that what gets "centralized upwards" in the absolutist state is not the feudal *fusion* of political and economic spheres but rather the politico-legal or coercive moment of feudalism as distinct from the moment of economic exploitation. The absolutist state simply represents for him the politico-legal coercive power which enforces the economic exploitation that takes place on a different plane.

In effect, the displacement upward of feudal political power plays the same role in Anderson's argument as the removal of fetters does in other versions of the old model. In fact, it seems that absolutism is one, if not *the,* essential means by which the fetters of feudalism were removed from the economy. Absolutism, then, seems to have been a necessary transitional point between feudalism and capitalism. In any case, freed from direct political bondage, commodity production was able to grow, and the "economy" could follow its own inclinations. Capitalism was the result of liberating the economy, removing the dead hand of feudalism, and unleashing the natural bearers of economic rationality, the burghers or bourgeois.

There are certain serious empirical problems in this treatment of absolutism as an apparently essential phase in the transition from feudalism to capitalism. Not the least of these problems is the fact that English capitalism did not enjoy the benefit of absolutism, while French absolutism did not give rise to capitalism (about which more in Part Two). If that is so, then it may be more plausible to argue that absolutism was not a transitional phase between feudalism and capitalism, but was, on the contrary, an alternative route out of feudalism. At any rate, it should at least be clear that in many fundamental ways, Anderson's account, like earlier explanations of the transition to capitalism, relies above all on the removal of fetters from a social form that already existed— more or less unexplained—within the interstices of feudalism.

For all the sophisticated complexity of Anderson's argument, it is a refinement—fascinating and in many ways illuminating, but no less a refinement—of the commercialization model. Echoes of that old explanation are even more audible in Anderson's most recent statement of his argument, in a review of Robert Brenner's book, *Merchants and Revolution.* Anderson is commenting here on Brenner's account of capitalism as, in the first instance, a specifically English phemonenon:

> The idea of capitalism in one country, taken literally, is only a bit more plausible than that of socialism. For Marx the different moments of the modern biography of capital were distributed in cumulative sequence, from the Italian cities to the towns of Flanders and Holland, to the empires of Portugal or Spain and the ports of France, before being 'systematically combined in England at the end of the 17th century.' Historically, it makes better sense to view the emergence of capitalism as a value-added process gaining in complexity as it moved along a chain of inter-related sites. In this story, the role of cities was always central. English landowners could never have started their conversion to commercial agriculture without the market for wool in Flemish towns—just as Dutch farming was by Stuart times in advance of English, not least because it was conjoined to a richer urban society.[15]

We should first take note that Marx, in the passage cited by Anderson, is explaining the "genesis of the *industrial* capitalist," not the origins of *capitalism,* the emergence of specifically capitalist "laws of motion," specifically capitalist social relations, a specifically capitalist form of exploitation, or the imperatives of self-sustaining growth.[16] Marx is trying to explain how the accumulation of wealth was converted in the right conditions—that is, in already capitalist social conditions (in England)—from simply the unproductive profits of usury and commerce into industrial capital. As for the origins of the capitalist *system*, the "so-called primitive accumulation"—that is, in Marx's term, the expropriation of direct producers, in particular peasants—which gave rise to specifically capitalist social property relations and the dynamic associated with them, Marx situates it firmly in England and in the countryside. Here too the conditions emerged for the unprecedented kind of *internal* market that Marx regarded as the sine qua non of industrial capitalism. Like Brenner after him, Marx acknowledges the need to explain the distinctiveness of England's development. Not the least of England's specificities, as Brenner points out, is that while other centers of production even in the medieval period had experienced export booms, early modern England was unique in maintaining industrial growth even in the context of declining overseas markets.[17] In other words, capitalism *indeed* in one country, albeit within a network of international trade.

But there is no need to get distracted here by speculations about Marx's views on the relation between agrarian and industrial capitalism (or about the questions he left unanswered and, indeed, the inconsistencies he left unresolved). We might simply note that Anderson's observations here beg the question. It is one thing to say, for example, that English commercial agriculture presupposed the Flemish market for wool. It is quite another to explain how "commercial agriculture" became *capitalist* agriculture, how the *possibility of trade* became not only the *actuality* but the *necessity* of *competitive production*, how market *opportunities* became market *imperatives*, how this specific kind of agriculture set in train the development of a capitalist *system*. We can certainly say that the European trading system and European imperialism were necessary conditions of capitalism, but we cannot just assume that commerce and capitalism are one and the same, or that one passed into the other by a simple process of growth. Anderson has assumed the very thing that needs to be demonstrated, namely that commerce, or indeed production for the market (a widespread practice throughout much of recorded history), became capitalism by means of sheer expansion, which at some point achieved a critical mass. His argument, in other words, suffers from the very circularity that has always afflicted the commercialization model.

Chapter Three

Marxist Alternatives

WHAT THE TRANSITION DEBATE LEFT UNEXPLAINED AND unaddressed was how and in what circumstances producers became subject to market *imperatives*. The assumption always appeared to be that capitalism emerged when obstacles to the realization of market *opportunities* were removed. A further episode in the ongoing debate among Marxists, however, has taken up the challenge of the transition debate in an effort to explain the transition from feudalism to capitalism without reading capitalist principles back into pre-capitalist societies—without, that is, assuming the very thing that needs to be explained.

The Brenner Debate

Historian Robert Brenner initiated a debate in 1976 with an important article, "Agrarian Class Structure and Economic Development in Pre-Industrial Europe," published in the journal *Past and Present*.[1] That article took aim at two influential models of historical explanation. The first was the increasingly dominant demographic model according to which economic development in post-medieval Europe followed long-term cycles in population growth—what he called a secular Malthusianism. The second was the commercialization model.

Brenner attacked the very foundations of both these competing models. In particular, he emphasized their inability to account for the fact that very different, indeed opposite, effects were produced in different countries by the same factors, with varying consequences not only for income distribution between classes but also for long-term economic growth and the development of productive forces. These divergent effects of apparently similar causes—similar demographic patterns in one model, insertion in the same network of increasing trade in the other—were enough to put in question the status of these causes as independent variables and seriously weakened the explanatory force of the dominant models. In their place, Brenner offered a powerful alternative explanation for the unprecedented process of self-sustaining economic growth that established itself in early modern England. His explanation focused on the varying configurations of social property relations that determined the divergent effects, in different contexts, of other factors (whose importance he did not dismiss) such as demographic cycles or the expansion of trade.

Brenner was clearly influenced by Maurice Dobb and, in the terms of the original transition debate, he was clearly more on Dobb's side than on Sweezy's. At the same time, it can be argued that Brenner started with some of the same questions that had troubled Sweezy. Like Sweezy, he clearly believed that a model of transition in which two antagonistic modes of production confront each other is inappropriate in dealing with the transition from feudalism to capitalism. There was no capitalism, even in embryonic form, to challenge feudalism—and this applied not only to pre-capitalist forms of trade but to petty commodity production treated, in the manner of Dobb and Hilton, as a kind of proto-capitalism. He also took as his starting point the tenacity of feudalism, criticizing other accounts of the transition for neglecting the "internal logic and solidity" of pre-capitalist economies and proceeding as if economic actors will adopt capitalist strategies when given the chance—a criticism that applies not only to the commercialization model but, in some ways, even to the theory of rising petty commodity production.

Brenner, however, did not, like Sweezy, proceed by looking for some external impetus to the dissolution of feudalism (in the context of certain property relations, for example, trade could and did lead, he argued, to a *tightening,* rather than a loosening, of pre-capitalist property forms). Instead, like Dobb and Hilton, Brenner looked for a dynamic internal to feudalism. But here we come to a major difference between his approach and theirs: what he was explicitly looking for was an internal dynamic that did not presuppose an already existent capitalist logic.

Class struggle figures prominently in his argument, as it did in Dobb's and Hilton's, but with Brenner it is not a question of *liberating* an impulse toward capitalism. Instead, it is a matter of lords and peasants, in certain specific conditions peculiar to England, involuntarily setting in train a capitalist dynamic while acting, in class conflict with each other, to reproduce themselves *as they were.* The unintended consequence was a situation in which producers were subjected to market imperatives. So Brenner really did depart from the old model and its tendency to assume the very thing that needs to be explained.

Brenner's explanation has to do with the very specific conditions of English property relations, and he emphasizes not just the specificity of Europe in relation to other cases but the differences among various states in Europe. In other words, the distinctive conditions which, for example, Michael Mann attributes to Europe in general in the Middle Ages are, for Brenner, not enough to explain the development of capitalism, or the specificity of the process of self-sustaining economic growth that emerged in England. In fact, his argument makes it clear that the dissolution of feudalism had more than one outcome in Europe—in particular, capitalism in England and absolutism in France, an absolutism that was not, as it was for Perry Anderson, simply a transitional phase in a more or less unilinear path toward capitalism.

In England, an exceptionally large proportion of land was owned by landlords and worked by tenants whose conditions of tenure increasingly took the form of economic leases, with rents not fixed by law or custom but responsive to market conditions. It could even be said that there existed a market in leases. The conditions of tenure were such that growing numbers of tenants were subjected to market imperatives—not the *opportunity* to produce for the market and grow from petty producers into capitalists but the *need* to specialize for the market and to produce competitively—simply in order to guarantee access to the means of subsistence.

At the same time, landlords in England were also in a special position. Although they controlled a uniquely large proportion of the best land, they did not enjoy—and did not really need—the kinds of extra-economic powers on which, say, the French aristocracy depended for much of its wealth. The English ruling class was distinctive in its growing dependence on the *productivity* of their tenants, rather than on exerting coercive power to squeeze more surplus out of them.

In other words, English property relations had what Brenner calls their own distinctive "rules for reproduction." Both direct producers and landlords came to depend on the market in historically unprecedented ways, just to secure the conditions of their own self-reproduction. These rules produced their own distinctive laws of motion. The result was to set in train a new historical dynamic: an unprecented rupture with old Malthusian cycles, a process of self-sustaining growth, new competitive pressures which had their own effects on the need to increase productivity, reconfiguring and further concentrating landholding, and so on. This new dynamic is agrarian capitalism (which will be discussed in greater detail in Part Two), and it was specific to England.

Although Brenner was clearly influenced by Dobb and Hilton, the difference between his argument and theirs should by now be clear. The operative principle in his argument is compulsion or imperative, not opportunity. If, for example, the petty commodity producer or yeoman farmer plays a major role here, it is not as the agent of an opportunity but as the subject of an imperative. Yeomen were typically the very kind of capitalist tenants who were subject to competitive pressures, and even owner-occupiers would be subject to those pressures once the competitive productivity of agrarian capitalism set the terms of economic survival. Both landlords and tenants came to depend on success in the market, as the former relied on the profits of the latter for their rents. Both had an interest in agricultural "improvement," the enhancement of productivity by means of innovative land use and techniques, which often implied, among other things, enclosure—not to mention the increasing exploitation of wage labor.

In a sense, Brenner also answered Sweezy's question about the "really revolutionary way." The capitalist tenant in England was not just a petty producer who had grown into a capitalist. His specific relation to the means of production, the conditions in which he had access to land itself, in a sense made him a capitalist *from the start*—that is, he became a capitalist not just because he had grown to some appropriate size or level of prosperity, not even just because his relative wealth allowed him to employ wage labor (non-capitalist farmers even in the ancient world were known to employ wage labor), but because his relations to the means of his own self-reproduction from the start subjected him, together with any wage laborers he may have employed, to market imperatives. Brenner's argument also lends support of a kind to Sweezy's contention that the transition from feudalism to capitalism was fueled not by the power of feudal lords to over-exploit but by the weaknesses in their ability to squeeze their peasants:

while England's uniquely centralized and unitary state guaranteed the English landlord's position and property when his feudal powers proved inadequate, the same conditions—which implied an unusually clear separation between state and "civil society," or between political and economic spheres—deprived him of extra-economic, coercive powers of surplus extraction and made him increasingly reliant on purely "economic" means of exploitation.

There have been various criticisms of Brenner, and some of the local disagreements about specific historical points are no doubt well-taken. But let me just briefly outline some of the more general criticisms that have implications for the larger issues in the transition debate.

Brenner's critique of earlier explanations had been, above all, that they took as given precisely those features of capitalism that require explanation, invoking, in circular fashion, some kind of pre-existing capitalism in order to explain the *emergence* of capitalism. The criticisms levelled against him in *The Brenner Debate* tended to repeat that mistake, not really defending so much as simply reproducing the presuppositions he had challenged. His critics, including both demographic historians and some Marxists, argued against him from a vantage point that took for granted the very aspects of capitalism he had sought to explain.

So, for example, the dean of demographic historians, Emmanuel Le Roy Ladurie, attacked Brenner for conflating economic and political factors by talking about "surplus-extracting" classes and "ruling" classes as if they were one and the same. Similarly, a Marxist historian, Guy Bois, took exception to the "voluntarism" of Brenner's "political Marxism," which, he maintained, neglected economic factors altogether. The latter account of Brenner's argument seemed to be reinforced in the introduction to the volume by R. H. Hilton, who (in diplomatic and more or less coded disagreement with Brenner) presented the issue between the varieties of Marxism represented respectively by Bois and Brenner as having to do with the relative weight given to *forces* as distinct from *relations* of production, the *"whole* mode of production" as distinct from just class conflict, economic factors as distinct from simply political ones. Hilton, despite his own tremendous contribution to the history of class struggle, seemed to be hinting that Brenner had leaned too much in the "politicist" direction.

The criticisms levelled by Bois and Le Roy Ladurie were quite substantially beside the point, and both were criticizing Brenner from a vantage point that took for granted a separation between the "political" and the "economic" that is specific to capitalism. Brenner's whole argument was predicated on the important observation, proposed originally by Marx, that pre-capitalist societies were characterized by "extra-economic" forms of surplus extraction, carried out by means of political, juridical, and military power, or what Brenner now calls "politically constituted property." In such cases, direct producers—notably peasants, who remained in possession of the means of production—were compelled by the superior force of their overlords to give up some of their surplus labor in the form of rent or tax. In the case of European feudalism in particular, lordship (as we saw in the discussion of Anderson) represented a *unity* of political and economic power. This is in sharp contrast to capitalism, where surplus extraction is purely "economic," achieved through the medium of commodity exchange as propertyless workers, responding to purely "economic" coercions, sell their labor power for a wage in order to gain access to the means of production. Following this insight to its logical conclusion, Brenner was neither, as Le Roy Ladurie complained, simplistically amalgamating economic and political factors nor, as Bois maintained, "privileging" political as against economic factors in his explanation of the transition from feudalism. Instead, he was exploring the consequences of the *fusion* of the "economic" and the "political," the unity of "surplus-extracting" and "ruling" classes, which was, precisely, a constitutive feature of the feudal mode of production.

Nor was it a matter of neglecting the technical forces of production. Brenner was simply building on the fundamental difference between the capitalist mode of appropriation, which depends on improving labor productivity because of the imperatives of competition and profit maximization—and hence encourages the improvement of productive forces—and pre-capitalist modes of appropriation. These earlier modes were not driven by the same requirement to improve the productivity of labor because surplus appropriation by dominant classes depended not on increasing the productivity of the direct producers but on strengthening the appropriator's coercive power to squeeze more surplus labor out of the producers. Brenner's principal questions, then, were these: how was it that old forms of "politically constituted property" were replaced in England by a purely "economic" form, and how did this set in train a distinctive pattern of self-sustaining economic growth?

Since *The Brenner Debate*, other criticisms have surfaced. First, there is a general criticism of the very idea that English agrarian relations were distinctive enough—in the seventeenth or even the eighteenth century—to justify calling them agrarian capitalism. There are two different kinds of arguments against the idea of agrarian capitalism. One has to do with whether English economic growth really was distinctive, whether, in particular, English agriculture even in the *eighteenth* century was distinct, specifically in its drive to improve productivity. Why, for example, some critics have asked, was French agricultural productivity in the eighteenth century roughly equivalent to that of English agriculture?[2] The second objection has to do with wage labor: since capitalism is defined, above all, by the exploitation of wage labor, some critics say, is it not a decisive argument against the concept of agrarian capitalism—or at least against its existence in the seventeenth century—that England was not yet a predominantly wage-earning society, that permanent and regular wage laborers were still very much in the minority?[3] What about the processes of expropriation and proletarianization, the differentiation of the English peasantry into prosperous farmers on the one hand and a propertyless class on the other? Do these processes not belong to the *pre*-history of capitalism?

These objections are revealing, but they may reveal more about the critics than about Brenner or the concept of agrarian capitalism. The first objection—about agricultural productivity in France—misses the point. It turns out that what these critics mean is that French agricultural production in the eighteenth century was roughly equivalent to English agriculture in its *total output*. But consider the fact that it took a much smaller rural population and a much smaller number of people engaged in agricultural production to produce that output in England than in France. This means that the so-called equivalence of French and English productivity—better to call it *production*—far from challenging the distinctiveness of English property relations and agrarian capitalism, actually confirms it. These same distinctive conditions created both a potential non-agricultural labor force and a potential mass market for cheap consumer goods like food and textiles, which were necessary conditions for the development of *industrial* capitalism.

How, then, is Brenner's argument affected by the other question, about the extent of wage labor? The problem here is not only an empirical one. We can agree that the extent of wage labor was limited in early modern England, especially regular and permanent—as distinct from casual or seasonal—wage labor. And we can agree that the process of expropriation and proletarianization was, by definition, absolutely central to the story of capitalism. But here, too, there is a begging of the question, and here again Brenner sets out to explain what others have taken for granted.

Brenner does not assume that a pre-existing division between rich and poor peasants such as has existed at other times and places would inevitably lead to polarization into rich farmers and dispossessed laborers. For example, both England and France in the later fifteenth century possessed a middle peasantry with relatively large holdings. (It might be added here that even in the sixteenth century, agricultural productivity in the two cases was not yet clearly different either.) Yet from this common starting point, they diverged in substantially different historical directions, the French toward increasing morcellization of peasant holdings, the English toward the agrarian triad of landlord, capitalist tenant, and wage laborer; the English toward agricultural improvement, the French toward agricultural stagnation.

Brenner has been accused of neglecting the role of small and middling farmers in the rise of capitalism and of writing a history of capitalism "from above."[4] But in his argument, it is neither landlords nor middling farmers nor, indeed, any other single class whose agency explains the rise of capitalism. It is rather a particular system of class *relations,* within which the participants acted to reproduce themselves *as they were,* with the unintended consequence of setting off a process of development that gave rise to capitalism.

It is certainly true, as some Marxist historians have argued, that the development of English capitalism required the development of fairly prosperous "middling" farmers and that yeomen played a leading role in the history of capitalism. It is, however, another matter to suggest that, once small commodity producers had thrown off the feudal fetters preventing them from growing into larger commodity producers prosperous enough to employ wage labor, the advent of capitalism was more or less guaranteed. This is where Brenner departs from his predecessors. The first point that comes immediately to mind here is that richer peasants have existed at many times and in many places—without becoming capitalists. Thus it must be asked why richer peasants in England began to behave in ways substantially different from any other prosperous peasants throughout recorded history, why English yeomen were not like Russian kulaks, or indeed like large tenant farmers in France at the same time. That difference and the reasons for it are precisely what Brenner has sought to explain.

Brenner does not assume that the English ruling class could simply have expropriated small farmers by brute force, or that they would have done so even if they could, in the absence of very specific economic conditions that made the dispossession of small producers not only possible but profitable. Brenner's explanation of the differentiation of the English peasantry (the "rise of the yeoman") which eventually ended in a polarization between capitalist farmers and propertyless laborers, again, has to do with the new economic logic that subjected English farmers to the imperatives of competition in unprecedented ways and degrees. This logic was imposed on farmers whether or not they consistently employed wage labor. It applied even when the tenant was himself, or together with his family, the direct producer.

This is a particularly important point: Brenner makes it clear that direct producers could be deprived of non-market access to the means of their own self-reproduction even while remaining in possession of the means of production, and that such a condition subjected them to the demands of the market. To reiterate the indispensable contrast we have been drawing here, peasants elsewhere and at other times had availed themselves of market *opportunities*, but English farmers were distinctive in their degree of subjection to market *imperatives*.

Brenner set out to explain why and how this came to be so, how producers were deprived of non-market access to the means of their self-reproduction and even to land itself, how landlordly forms of exploitation were transformed from "extra-economic" surplus extraction to the appropriation of capitalist rents, how it came about that both landlords and tenants were compelled and enabled to move in response to the imperatives of competition, how new forms of appropriation established new compulsions, and how those compulsions conditioned the differentiation— and in large part the dispossession—of the peasantry. This happened through purely "economic" pressures of competition no less than through more direct coercion by landlords with a new kind of economic interest in large and concentrated holdings. A mass proletariat was the *end,* not the beginning, of the process. It cannot be emphasized enough that for Brenner, the market dependence of economic actors was a *cause,* not a result, of proletarianization.

The great strength of Brenner's argument is that it emphasizes the specificity of the historical process that brought capitalism into being, with its new and historically specific economic logic, and that he makes a convincing effort to explain how it came about. Many historians have claimed to be explaining the transition from feudalism to capitalism. But in their various ways, most attempts to explain the process of transition tend to generalize laws of motion specific to capitalism and turn them into universal principles of historical movement. Even when such attempts acknowledge the particularity of capitalism as a specific historical form, the emergence of that historical form takes place by means of essentially capitalist processes. Brenner is one of a very few writers who actually do deal with a *process* of transition, the transformation of one kind of society into another, one set of rules for reproduction to another, even one historical dynamic to another.

Brenner and "Bourgeois Revolution"

One final criticism of Brenner is especially revealing. Some years after the original Brenner debate, Brenner published *Merchants and Revolution* (1993), a major study of early modern England which considered the role of merchants in the English Revolution. Several critics quickly seized on the fact that Brenner was attributing an important revolutionary role to merchants. After insisting that capitalism was born in the countryside, they argued, Brenner has had to acknowledge the bourgeoisie and bourgeois revolution after all.

Among the foremost exponents of this view was Perry Anderson. There is, he argued in a review of the book, a "deep paradox" in Brenner's work, a fundamental contradiction between his original thesis on the origin of capitalism and his latest work on merchants:

> Here, if ever, were revolutionary bourgeois. The species declared a fiction in France was *bel et bien* a reality in England, a hundred years before the Convention. There is a nice irony that it should be massive historical evidence, running against—not with—a theoretical conviction which has brought a Marxist scholar to this conclusion. The detractor of the significance of merchant capital in principle has been the first to establish, in spell-binding detail, its role as a demi-urge in practice.[5]

Brenner, it must first be said, has conceded nothing of the kind. But to understand the significance of his argument, we need to situate it in the context of his views on "bourgeois revolution." There is no question that he has issued a challenge to conventional Marxist historiography on this score, strongly suggesting that its conception of bourgeois revolution has much in common with the commercialization model.

The traditional conception of bourgeois revolution, he argued, belongs to a phase of Marx's work still heavily dependent upon the mechanical materialism of the eighteenth-century Enlightenment and contrasts sharply with Marx's mature critique of political economy.[6] In the earlier theory, productive forces develop almost naturally via the division of labor, which in turn evolves in response to expanding markets, so that the pre-existence of capitalism is invoked in order to explain its coming into being. The traditional conception of bourgeois revolution as an account of the transition to capitalism is, then, self-contradictory and self-defeating, because on its own assumptions, "it renders revolution doubly unnecessary":

First, there is no *transition* to accomplish, really: since the model starts with bourgeois society in the towns, foresees its evolution taking place by way of bourgeois mechanisms, and has feudalism transcend itself in consequence of its exposure to trade, the problem of how one type of society is transformed into another is simply assumed away and never posed. Second, since bourgeois society self-develops and dissolves feudalism, the bourgeois revolution can hardly claim a necessary role.[7]

Having argued that the thesis of bourgeois revolution, like the old commercialization model, assumed the very thing that needed to be explained by attributing to the bourgeoisie a capitalist rationality that had only to be released from the bonds of feudalism, Brenner opened the way for a thorough reassessment of the bourgeoisie and its role in the rise of capitalism. This is the background to his account of London merchants, and especially the book's lengthy postscript. The charge that he has undermined his own original thesis simply replicates the circular and question-begging logic which that thesis was designed to correct.

The point is nowhere better illustrated than in Perry Anderson's "deep paradox." His criticism, it can be argued, is every bit as question-begging as the old commercialization model, and it draws our attention to one very important consequence of that model: the long-standing tendency to equate "bourgeois" with "capitalist."

We may be utterly convinced that, say, the French Revolution was thoroughly bourgeois, indeed much more so than the English, without coming a flea-hop closer to determining whether it was also *capitalist*. As long as we accept that there is no necessary identification of *bourgeois* (or *burgher* or *city*) with *capitalist*, the revolutionary bourgeois can be far from a fiction, even—or especially—in France, where the model revolutionary bourgeois was not a capitalist or even an old-fashioned merchant but a lawyer or officeholder. At the same time, if the revolutionary bourgeois in England *was* inextricably linked with capitalism, it is precisely because capitalist social property relations had already been established in the English countryside.

There is, of course, much that Brenner does not do. One especially important point demanding exploration is that, although the commercialization model may be fatally flawed, this does not change the fact that capitalism emerged within a network of international trade and could not have emerged without that network. So a great deal still needs to be said about how England's particular insertion into the international trading system determined the development of English capitalism. England arguably transformed the nature of trade by creating a distinctive *national* market, in fact the first national market (centered on London), and perhaps the first truly competitive market. Much still needs to be learned about how this affected the nature of *international* trade.

Another big issue is the European state system and its contribution to the development of English capitalism. Together the system of trade and the state system operated as the conduit through which England was eventually able to transmit its competitive pressures to other states and economies, so that *non*-capitalist states could become engines of capitalist development in response to these external pressures.[8] We have hardly begun to explore the mechanisms by which capitalism imposed its imperatives on other European states, and eventually on the whole world. This would also have to play a major part in explaining how capitalism has transformed traditional forms of colonialism into a new, capitalist form of imperialism. A systematic explaining of these historical questions might, among other things, be a big help in dealing with the so-called globalization process today.

E. P. Thompson

Brenner's argument, by showing how direct producers became subject to market imperatives, even if it does not explicate the role of towns and markets in the development of capitalism, explains the context in which the very nature of trade and markets was transformed, acquiring an entirely new economic role and a new systemic logic. This happened long before industrialization and was a precondition to it. Market imperatives, in other words, imposed themselves on direct producers before the mass proletarianization of the work force. They were a decisive factor in creating a mass proletariat, as market forces, supported by direct coercion in the form of political and judicial intervention, created a propertyless majority.

How the imperatives of the market established themselves in the period leading up to industrialization has been most vividly described by E. P. Thompson. In his work, the development of capitalism comes to life not only as a process of proletarianization, particularly in his classic work *The Making of the English Working Class* (1963), but also as a living confrontation between market principles and alternative practices and values. The implantation of "market society" emerges as a confrontation between classes, between those whose interests were expressed in the new political economy of the market and those who contested it by putting the right of subsistence before the imperatives of profit.

In the central section of *The Making of the English Working Class* entitled "Exploitation," Thompson outlines what for him are the pivotal moments in the emergence of industrial capitalism. Two related points stand out in his analysis. The first is the timing of the transformative moment, the "making" of a new working class. Thompson situates the transforming experience of the English working class, the process in which a new proletariat and a new working class culture were forged, in the period 1790-1832. His analysis therefore ends well before the industrial transformation of production was complete or even very far advanced. The second, related point is that he sees a transformation in what appears to be a fundamental continuity: even workers who, on the face of it, seem hardly different from their artisanal predecessors, and whose oppositional culture is still deeply rooted in old pre-industrial popular and radical traditions, are, for Thompson, a "fresh race of beings," a new kind of proletariat.

Some Marxist critics of Thompson have interpreted these striking features as evidence of Thompson's preoccupation with "subjective," cultural factors, at the expense of "objective" changes in the mode of production itself, specifically, the transformative effects of technological change on the organization of production and on the nature of the labor force.[9] But here again, Marxist critics may be conceding too much to standard histories of capitalist development. The tendency among historians of various ideological persuasions has been to trace the causes of the "Industrial Revolution"—if they accept the notion of an industrial revolution at all—to technical innovations or developments in trade and market relations. Thompson, by contrast, like Brenner after him, is doing something rather more subtle and complex—following, it can be argued, the principles (if not always the practice) of Marx himself. For all the many differences in style and subject matter between Brenner and Thompson, it is possible to imagine an account of industrialization building upon Brenner's challenge to conventional ideas about capitalist development that would have more in common with Thompson's history than with any other.

Brenner, readers will remember, sought to account for the emergence of new "rules for reproduction." He showed that the dynamic of self-sustaining growth, and the constant need for improvement in labor productivity, presupposed transformations in property relations that created a need for such improvements simply to permit the principal economic actors—landlords and peasants—to reproduce themselves. The differences between England and France, for example, had little to do in the first instance with any differences in their respective technological capacities. They were distinguished by the nature of relations between landlords and peasants: one case demanded enhancement of labor productivity, the other did not. The systematic drive to revolutionize the forces of production was result more than cause.

Thompson's account of industrialization is rooted in the same perception. His purpose is to explore the consequences of specifically capitalist modes of exploitation. Among those consequences in the period of transition to industrial capitalism was the intensification of labor and work discipline. What created the drive to intensify exploitation was not the emergence of steam or the factory system but rather the need inherent in capitalist property relations to increase productivity and profit. Those capitalist imperatives were imposed on traditional forms of work no less than on new forms of labor, on artisans still engaged in pre-industrial production no less than on factory hands. "Large-scale sweated outwork was," Thompson argues, "as intrinsic to this revolution as was factory production and steam."[10] A common experience of capitalist imperatives and capitalist exploitation is what made it possible for diverse kinds of workers to join in class organizations and create a new kind of working-class culture. To be sure, these imperatives were bound to transform the organization of production and the nature of the working class, but the factory system was result more than cause.

Here Thompson is pursuing the distinction made by Marx between the "formal" and the "real" subsumption of labor by capital. In the first instance, capital appropriated surplus labor from workers still engaged in traditional forms of production. This form of exploitation was driven by capitalist imperatives, its imperatives of competition and accumulation, but those imperatives did not at first transform the technical process of production. We may want to say that capitalism did not reach maturity until capital had transformed the labor process itself specifically to meet the needs of capital—that is, until capitalism assumed its industrial form. But we can nonetheless recognize that industrial capitalism was the result, not the cause, of capitalist laws of motion.

So the answer to those like Perry Anderson who have wondered why Thompson, after *The Making of the English Working Class*, moved back into the eighteenth century instead of forward, beyond the 1830s to a fuller account of industrialization, is that he was trying to explain the establishment of *capitalism* as a social form, not some neutral technical process called "industrialization." He was particularly interested in the eighteenth century as the moment when the capitalist transformation of property relations was being consolidated and was playing itself out in the articulation of a new capitalist ideology more self-conscious and explicit than ever before. It was also a moment when the new economic principles had not yet taken full shape as a hegemonic ideology, the political economy of the market, which would soon infiltrate even some of the most radical opposition to capitalism.

Thompson suggests that in eighteenth-century England the market was in fact the main arena of struggle. This was so for reasons very specific to this transitory moment in English history. On the one hand, this was a moment of "free" labor, subject neither to pre-capitalist, extra-economic forms of domination nor as yet, in general, to the new disciplines of the factory, so that people for a short time still controlled "their own immediate relations and modes of work." On the other hand, "they had very little control over the market for their products or over the prices of raw materials or food." This is why social protest was so often directed at the market. People, often women, opposed not only what they regarded as unjust prices but illegitimate and immoral market practices—practices designed to increase profit, which from the vantage point of market society and capitalist rationality seem perfectly normal today but which violated certain customary expectations about rights of access to the means of life.[11]

In some of these protests, we can also see opposition to the transformation of the market from a visible, more or less transparent, institution into an "invisible hand." The market people were most familiar with was a physical place where people put commodities on offer for other people to buy, according to principles governed to some extent by custom, communal regulation, and expectations about the right to subsistence. Now it was becoming a mechanism beyond communal control, as the transparency of market transactions was supplanted by the mysteries of a "self-regulating" market, the price mechanism, and the subordination of all communal values to the imperatives of profit.

Thompson also shows how the new ideology of political economy, including new conceptions of property and the ethic of profit, was increasingly enforced by state repression. The courts would put the proprietor's right to profit by increasing productivity above other kinds of right, such as the customary use rights long enjoyed by non-owners, or the right to subsistence. And the civil authority reacted more violently, especially in the wake of the French Revolution, to protest against unjust prices and market practices. Coercion by the state, in other words, was required to impose the coercion of the market.

Summing Up

So far the argument of this book has been that the main problem in most standard histories of capitalism is that they start—or end—with concepts that obscure the specificity of capitalism. We need a form of history that brings this specificity into sharp relief, one that acknowledges the difference between commercial profit-taking and capitalist accumulation, between the market as an opportunity and the market as an imperative, and between transhistorical processes of technological development and the specific capitalist drive to improve labor productivity. We need to trace these specificities of capitalism to their roots in forms of property and class relations. Most Marxists would no doubt claim to be doing all or most of these things, but I have tried to show that their accounts of history with very few exceptions fail to proceed consistently on that basis, with the consequence that the specificity of capitalism remains disguised.

It is worth adding that the question-begging assumptions of the old commercialization model can appear in the most unlikely places. For example, critics who accuse historians, and often Western Marxists in particular, of being "Eurocentric" may, paradoxically, be reproducing the very assumption that makes the commercialization model the most Eurocentric of all. That model, again, was based on the premise that Europe deserves the credit for lifting barriers to the natural development of capitalism, permitting it to grow to maturity from its origins in urban society and trade. At least some anti-Eurocentric arguments proceed by challenging European primacy in that achievement. But it is hard to see the advantage of arguing that non-European societies with more highly developed urban civilizations and trading systems were further down the road of capitalist development than is acknowledged by Eurocentric versions of the model. That seems a peculiarly ineffective challenge to the old model and its naturalization of capitalism, accepting that model's very first premise. More particularly, such arguments tend to reinforce the deeply Eurocentric view that the absence of capitalism is somehow a historic failure (an especially counterproductive line of thought for *critics* of capitalism).

A more challenging anti-Eurocentric criticism concerns the neglect by many Western historians of the role played by European imperialism in the development of capitalism. But such an argument can be truly effective only if it takes into account the very specific conditions in which traditional forms of colonialism were transformed into capitalist imperialism. And that means acknowledging the very specific conditions in which social property relations assumed a capitalist form in the first place.

On the face of it, much has happened in historical scholarship since the commercialization model first emerged. Some of the most well-established conventions of Western historiography have been challenged and ostensibly subverted at their very foundations—not only by Marxists but by "revisionist" historians of one kind or another, postmodernists, and other iconoclasts. Yet it is a measure of how deeply rooted the old question-begging explanations of capitalism are that they are still present in the most current scholarship—for instance, in today's conceptions of modernity and postmodernity—and in our conventional everyday language, which still identifies *capitalist* with *bourgeois,* and both with *modernity.*

Part Two

The Origin of Capitalism

Chapter Four

The Agrarian Origin of Capitalism

THE EMERGENCE OF CAPITALISM CERTAINLY PRESUPPOSED Western feudalism, not to mention the development of certain property forms in Graeco-Roman antiquity.[1] But it is one thing to say that European feudalism was a *necessary* condition for the emergence of capitalism (as, indeed, were other factors, such as the existence of a trading network that included a world far beyond Western Europe), and quite another to say that it was *sufficient*. Feudalism in Europe, even in Western Europe, was internally diverse, and it produced several different outcomes, only one of which was capitalism. It is not just a matter of different rates of "combined and uneven development" or even of different transitional phases. The autonomous city-states that emerged in Renaissance Italy, for example, or the absolutist state in France, were distinct formations, each with its own internal logic of process which need not have given rise to capitalism. Where and when they did issue in capitalism, it was only as they came within the orbit of an already existing capitalist system and the competitive pressures it was able to impose on its political, military, or commercial rivals. No entry into the capitalist economy could thereafter be the same as earlier ones, as they all became subject to a larger and increasingly international capitalist system.[2]

The tendency to take for granted that capitalism was an inevitable, if antagonistic, outgrowth of European feudalism is, as we have seen, rooted in the conviction that the autonomous town which grew within the interstices of feudalism's "parcellized sovereignties" was not only the natural enemy that would destroy the feudal system but the "cuckoo's egg" within it that would give birth to capitalism. To detach ourselves from that presupposition means, first, to disentangle *capitalist* from *bourgeois,* and *capitalism* from the *city.*

Agrarian Capitalism

The association of capitalism with cities is one of the most well-established conventions of Western culture. Capitalism is supposed to have been born and bred in the city. But more than that, the implication is that *any* city—with its characteristic practices of trade and commerce—is by its very nature potentially capitalist from the start, and only extraneous obstacles have stood in the way of *any* urban civilization giving rise to capitalism. Only the wrong religion, the wrong kind of state, or other ideological, political, or cultural fetters tying the hands of urban classes have prevented capitalism from springing up anywhere and everywhere, since time immemorial—or at least since technology has permitted the production of adequate surpluses.

What accounts for the development of capitalism in the West, according to this view, is the unique autonomy of its cities and of their quintessential class, the burghers or bourgeois. In other words, capitalism emerged in the West less because of what was present than because of what was absent: constraints on urban economic practices. In those conditions, it took only a more or less natural expansion of trade to trigger the development of capitalism to its full maturity. All that was needed was a quantitative growth which occurred almost inevitably with the passage of time (in some versions, of course, helped along, but not originally caused, by the "Protestant ethic").

There are many questionable things in these assumptions about the natural connection between cities and capitalism, but foremost among them must be the tendency to naturalize capitalism, to disguise its distinctiveness as a historically specific social form with a beginning and, potentially, an end. The tendency to identify capitalism with cities and urban commerce has, as we have seen, generally been accompanied by an inclination to make capitalism appear a more or less automatic consequence of practices as old as human history, or even the consequence of a "natural" inclination, in Adam Smith's words, to "truck, barter, and exchange."

Perhaps the most salutary corrective to these assumptions and their ideological implications is the recognition that capitalism, with all its very specific drives of accumulation and profit maximization, was born not in the city but in the countryside, in a very specific place, and very late in human history. It required not a simple extension or expansion of barter and exchange but a complete transformation in the most basic human relations and practices, a rupture in age-old patterns of human interaction with nature.

For millennia, human beings have provided for their material needs by working the land. And probably for nearly as long as they have engaged in agriculture they have been divided into classes, between those who worked the land and those who appropriated the labor of others. That division between appropriators and producers has taken many forms, but one common characteristic is that the direct producers have typically been peasants. These peasant producers have remained in possession of the means of production, specifically land. As in all pre-capitalist societies, these producers have had direct access to the means of their own reproduction. This has meant that when their surplus labor has been appropriated by exploiters, it has been done by what Marx called "extra-economic" means—that is, by means of direct coercion, exercised by landlords or states employing their superior force, their privileged access to military, judicial, and political power.

Here, then, is the basic difference between all pre-capitalist societies and capitalism. It has nothing to do with whether production is urban or rural and everything to do with the particular property relations between producers and appropriators, whether in industry or agriculture. Only in capitalism is the dominant mode of appropriation based on the dispossession of the legally free direct producers, whose surplus labor is appropriated by purely "economic" means. Because direct producers in a fully developed capitalism are propertyless, and because their only access to the means of production, to the requirements of their own reproduction, even to the means of their own labor, is the sale of their labor power in exchange for a wage, capitalists can appropriate the workers' surplus labor without direct coercion.

This unique relation between producers and appropriators is, of course, mediated by the "market." Markets of various kinds have existed throughout recorded history and no doubt before, as people have exchanged and sold their surpluses in many different ways and for many different purposes. But the market in capitalism has a distinctive, unprecedented function. Virtually everything in capitalist society is a commodity produced for the market. And even more fundamentally, both capital and labor are utterly dependent on the market for the most basic conditions of their own reproduction. Just as workers depend on the market to sell their labor power as a commodity, capitalists depend on it to buy labor power, as well as the means of production, and to realize their profits by selling the goods or services produced by the workers. This market dependence gives the market an unprecedented role in capitalist societies, as not only a simple mechanism of exchange or distribution but the principal determinant and regulator of social reproduction. The emergence of the market as a determinant of social reproduction presupposed its penetration into the production of life's most basic necessity: food.

This unique system of market dependence entails specific systemic requirements and compulsions shared by no other mode of production: the imperatives of competition, accumulation, and profit maximization. And these imperatives, in turn, mean that capitalism can and must constantly expand in ways and degrees unlike any other social form. It can and must constantly accumulate, constantly search out new markets, constantly impose its imperatives on new territories and new spheres of life, on all human beings and the natural environment.

Once we recognize just how distinctive these social relations and processes are, how different they are from the social forms which have dominated most of human history, it becomes clear that more is required to explain the emergence of this distinctive social form than the question-begging assumption that it has always existed in embryo, just needing to be liberated from unnatural constraints. The question of its origins can be formulated this way: given that producers were exploited by appropriators in non-capitalist ways for millennia before the advent of capitalism, and given that markets have also existed "time out of mind" and almost everywhere, how did it happen that producers and appropriators, and the relations between them, came to be so market dependent?

Now obviously the long and complex historical processes that ultimately led to this condition of market dependence could be traced back indefinitely. But we can make the question more manageable by identifying the first time and place that a new social dynamic of market dependence is clearly discernible.

Even later than the seventeenth century, most of the world, including Europe, was free of the market-driven imperatives outlined here. A vast system of trade certainly existed, extending across the globe. But nowhere, neither in the great trading centers of Europe nor in the vast commercial networks of the Islamic world or Asia, was economic activity and production in particular driven by the imperatives of competition and accumulation. The dominant principle of trade everywhere was "buying cheap and selling dear."

International trade was essentially carrying trade, with merchants buying goods in one location to be sold for profit in another. But even within a single, powerful, and relatively unified European kingdom like France, basically the same principles of non-capitalist commerce prevailed. There was no single and unified market, a market in which people made profit not by buying cheap and selling dear, not by carrying goods from one market to another, but by producing more cost-effectively in direct competition with others in the same market.

Trade still tended to be in luxury goods, or at least goods destined for more prosperous households or answering to the needs and consumption patterns of dominant classes. There was no mass market for cheap everyday consumer products. Peasant producers would typically produce not only their own food but other everyday goods like clothing. They might take their surpluses to local markets, where the proceeds could be exchanged for other commodities. Farm produce might even be sold in markets further afield. But here again, the principles of trade were basically the same as in manufactured goods.

Here readers might recall Karl Polanyi's illuminating argument about trade before the advent of "market society," about its fundamentally non-competitive character. But let me clarify some points here, which may not be entirely clear in Polanyi's account. Take the example of long-distance trade, the particular form of economic activity that defined the great commercial centers which are, according to all versions of the commercialization model, supposed to have been the precursors of capitalism. This kind of trade took the form of "commercial arbitrage between separate markets."[3] Buying cheap in one market and selling dear in another was the operative principle here, not competition within a single, integrated market. If there was competition, it did not take the form of competitive and cost-effective production. Essentially "extra-economic" conditions, such as domination of the seas and other transport routes, or highly developed financial institutions and instruments of arbitrage, were the key to commercial advantage. This kind of trade, largely in luxury goods for a fairly limited market, did not in itself carry an impulse to improve productivity. The main vocation of the large merchant was circulation rather than production. Even when a major commercial center like Florence developed domestic production, in addition to its role in servicing external mercantile activity, the basic logic of economic transactions was not essentially different. It was still a matter of limited production for a luxury market and a recycling of wealth or "profit on alienation," in the process of circulation, rather than the creation of value in production, and appropriation of surplus value, in the capitalist manner.

These non-capitalist principles of trade existed in conjunction with non-capitalist modes of exploitation. For instance, in Western Europe, even where feudal serfdom had effectively disappeared, other forms of "extra-economic" exploitation still prevailed. In eighteenth-century France, for example, where peasants still constituted the vast majority of the population and remained in possession of most land, office in the central state served as an economic resource for many members of the dominant classes, a means of extracting surplus labor in the form of taxes from peasant producers. Even rent-appropriating landlords typically depended on various extra-economic powers and privileges to enhance their wealth.

So peasants had access to the means of production, the land, without having to offer their labor power as a market commodity. Landlords and officeholders, with the help of various "extra-economic" powers and privileges, extracted surplus labor from peasants directly in the form of rent or tax. While all kinds of people might buy and sell all kinds of things in the market, neither the peasant-proprietors who produced, nor the landlords and officeholders who appropriated what others produced, depended directly on the market for the conditions of their self-reproduction, and the relations between them were not mediated by the market.

But there was one major exception to this general rule. England, by the sixteenth century, was developing in wholly new directions. Although there were other relatively strong monarchical states in Europe, more or less unified under a monarchy, such as Spain and France, none was as effectively unified as England (and the emphasis here is on England, not other parts of the British Isles). In the eleventh century, when the Norman ruling class established itself on the island as a fairly cohesive military and political entity, England already became more unified than most countries. In the sixteenth century, England went a long way toward eliminating the fragmentation of the state, the "parcellized sovereignty," inherited from feudalism. The autonomous powers held by lords, municipal bodies, and other corporate entities in other European states were, in England, increasingly concentrated in the central state. This was in contrast to other European states where powerful monarchies continued for a long time to live uneasily alongside other post-feudal military powers, fragmented legal systems, and corporate privileges whose possessors insisted on their autonomy against the centralizing power of the state.

The distinctive political centralization of the English state had material foundations and corollaries. Already in the sixteenth century, England had an impressive network of roads and water transport that unified the nation to a degree unusual for the period. London, becoming disproportionately large in relation to other English towns and to the total population of England (and eventually the largest city in Europe), was also becoming the hub of a developing national market.

The material foundation on which this emerging national economy rested was English agriculture, which was unique in several ways. First, the English ruling class was distinctive in two related respects.[4] On the one hand, demilitarized before any other aristocracy in Europe, it was part of an increasingly centralized state, in alliance with a centralizing monarchy, without the parcellization of sovereignty characteristic of feudalism and its successor states. While the state served the ruling class as an instrument of order and protector of property, the aristocracy did not possess autonomous "extra-economic" powers or "politically constituted property" to the same degree as their continental counterparts.

On the other hand, there was what might be called a trade-off between the centralization of state power and the aristocracy's control of land. Land in England had for a long time been unusually concentrated, with big landlords holding an unusually large proportion. This concentrated landownership meant that English landlords were able to use their property in new ways. What they lacked in "extra-economic" powers of surplus extraction they more than made up for with increasing "economic" powers.

This distinctive combination had significant consequences. On the one hand, the concentration of English landholding meant that an unusually large proportion of land was worked not by peasant-proprietors but by tenants (the word "farmer," incidentally, literally means "tenant"—a usage suggested by phrases familiar today, such as "farming out"). This was true even before the waves of dispossession, especially in the sixteenth and eighteenth centuries, conventionally associated with "enclosure," and was in contrast, for example, to France, where a larger proportion of land remained, and would long continue to remain, in the hands of peasants.

On the other hand, the relatively weak extra-economic powers of landlords meant that they depended less on their ability to squeeze more rents out of their tenants by direct, coercive means than on their tenants' productivity. Agrarian landlords in this arrangement had a strong incentive to encourage—and, wherever possible, to compel—their tenants to find ways of increasing their output. In this respect, they were fundamentally different from rentier aristocrats who throughout history have depended for their wealth on squeezing surpluses out of peasants by means of simple coercion, enhancing their powers of surplus extraction not by increasing the productivity of the direct producers but rather by improving their own coercive powers—military, judicial, and political.

As for the tenants, they were increasingly subject not only to direct pressures from landlords but to market imperatives which compelled them to enhance their productivity. English tenancies took various forms, and there were many regional variations, but a growing number were subject to economic rents—rents fixed not by some legal or customary standard but by market conditions. There was, in effect, a market in leases. Tenants were obliged to compete not only in a market for consumers but in a market for access to land. Where security of tenure depended on the ability to pay the going rent, uncompetitive production could mean outright loss of land. To meet economic rents in a situation where other potential tenants were competing for the same leases, tenants were compelled to produce cost-effectively, on penalty of dispossession. The effect of the system of property relations was that many agricultural producers (including prosperous "yeomen") became market dependent in their access to land itself, to the means of production.

The development of these economic rents illustrates the difference between the market as opportunity and the market as imperative. It also exposes the deficiencies in accounts of capitalist development based on the conventional assumptions. The ways in which those assumptions have determined perceptions of the evidence is nicely illustrated in an important article from the transition debate on the structural role of towns in feudalism. John Merrington suggests that although the transformation of feudal surplus labor into monetary rents did not in itself alter the fundamental nature of feudal relations, it did have one important consequence: by helping to fix surplus labor to a constant magnitude it "stimulated the growth of independent commodity production."[5]

But this proposition seems to be based less on empirical evidence than on the market-as-opportunity model, with its assumption that petty producers would choose to act like capitalists if only given the chance. The effects of monetary rents varied widely according to the property relations between the peasants who produced those rents and the landlords who appropriated them. Where the extra-economic powers of feudal lords remained strong, peasants could be subjected to the same coercive pressures as before from landlords seeking to squeeze more surplus labor out of them, even if now it took the form of monetary rents instead of labor services. Where, as in France, the peasantry's hold on property was strong enough to resist such increasing pressures from landlords, rents were often fixed at a nominal rate. Surely it is precisely in a case like this, with peasants enjoying secure property rights and subject not only to fixed but modest rents, that we might, on the basis of Merrington's assumptions, expect to find a stimulus to commodity production that might eventually give rise to capitalism. But the effect was just the opposite. The evidence outlined by Brenner suggests that it was not fixed rents of this kind that stimulated the growth of commodity production. On the contrary, it was *unfixed, variable* rents responsive to market imperatives that in England stimulated the development of commodity production, the improvement of productivity, and self-sustaining economic growth. In France, precisely because peasants typically enjoyed possession of land at fixed and nominal rents, no such stimulus existed. It was, in other words, not the *opportunities* afforded by the market but rather its *imperatives* that drove petty commodity producers to accumulate.

By the early modern period, even many customary leases in England had effectively become economic leases of this kind. But even those tenants who enjoyed some kind of customary tenure which gave them more security, but who might still be obliged to sell their produce in the same markets, could go under in conditions where competitive standards of productivity were being set by farmers responding more directly and urgently to the pressures of the market. The same would increasingly be true even of landowners working their own land. In this competitive environment, productive farmers prospered and their holdings were likely to grow, while less competitive producers went to the wall and joined the propertyless classes.

Competitive market forces were, then, a major factor in expropriating direct producers. But these economic forces were, no doubt, assisted by direct coercive intervention to evict tenants or to extinguish their customary rights. Perhaps some historians have exaggerated the decline of the English peasantry, which may have taken much longer to disappear completely than some accounts suggest. But there can be little doubt that in comparison with other European peasantries, the English variety was a rare and endangered species, and market imperatives certainly accelerated the polarization of English rural society into larger landowners and a growing propertyless multitude. The famous triad of landlord, capitalist tenant, and wage-laborer was the result, and with the growth of wage labor the pressures to improve labor productivity also increased. The same process created a highly productive agriculture capable of sustaining a large population not engaged in agricultural production, but also an increasing propertyless mass which would constitute both a large wage-labor force and a domestic market for cheap consumer goods—a type of market with no historical precedent. This is the background to the formation of English industrial capitalism.

The effect of market imperatives was to intensify exploitation in order to increase productivity—whether exploitation of the labor of others or self-exploitation by the farmer and his family. This pattern would be reproduced in the British colonies, and indeed in early national America, where independent small farmers who were supposed to be the backbone of a free republic faced from the beginning the stark choice of agrarian capitalism: at best intense self-exploitation and at worst dispossession and displacement by larger, more productive enterprises.

The contrast with France is illuminating. The crisis of French feudalism was resolved by a different kind of state formation. Here, the aristocracy long retained its hold on politically constituted property, but when feudalism was replaced by absolutism, politically constituted property was not replaced by purely economic exploitation or capitalist production. Instead, the French ruling class gained new extra-economic powers as the absolutist state created a vast apparatus of office by means of which a section of the propertied class could appropriate the surplus labor of peasants in the form of tax. Even then, at the height of absolutism, France remained a confusing welter of competing jurisdictions, as nobility and municipal authorities clung to the remnants of their autonomous feudal powers, the residues of feudal "parcellized sovereignty." In these conditions, the preferred economic strategy was still to squeeze the peasants by extra-economic means rather than to encourage competitive production and "improvement." There was no impetus to capitalist development comparable to England's until England itself succeeded in imposing its competitive pressures on an international economy.

It is worth noting, too, that the integrated national market which Polanyi described as the first kind of market to operate on competitive principles developed in England long before anywhere else, while France had to await the Napoleonic era to remove internal barriers to trade. The important point is that the development of a competitive national market was a corollary, not a cause, of capitalism and market society. The evolution of a unified, competitive national market reflected changes in the mode of exploitation and the nature of the state.

So, for example, in France, the persistence of politically constituted property, or "extra-economic" forms of exploitation, meant that neither the state nor the economy was truly integrated. Powers of exploitation that were political and economic at the same time, in the form of state office as well as the remnants of old aristocratic and municipal jurisdictions, tended to fragment both state and economy even under absolutism. In England, there was a clearer separation between the political, coercive powers of the state and the exploitative powers of propertied classes which derived their wealth from purely "economic" forms of exploitation. So the private economic powers of the ruling class did not detract from the political unity of the state, and there was both a truly centralized state and an integrated national economy.

The Rise of Capitalist Property and the Ethic of "Improvement"

English agriculture, then, was already in the sixteenth century marked by a unique combination of conditions, at least in certain regions, which would gradually set the economic direction of the whole economy. The result was an agrarian sector more productive than any other in history. Landlords and tenants alike became preoccupied with what they called "improvement," the enhancement of the land's productivity for profit.

It is worth dwelling for a moment on this concept of improvement, because it tells us a great deal about English agriculture and the development of capitalism. The word "improve" itself, in its original meaning, did not mean just "make better" in a general sense but literally meant to do something for monetary profit, especially to cultivate land for profit (based on the old French for "into," *en,* and "profit," *pros*—or its oblique case, *preu).* By the seventeenth century, the word "improver" was firmly fixed in the language to refer to someone who rendered land productive and profitable, especially by enclosing it or reclaiming waste. Agricultural improvement was by then a well-established practice, and in the eighteenth century, in the golden age of agrarian capitalism, "improvement" in word and deed came truly into its own.

The word was at the same time acquiring a more general meaning in the sense that we know it today (we might like to think about the implications of a culture in which the word for "making better" is rooted in the word for monetary profit). Even in its association with agriculture, it eventually lost some of its old specificity—so that, for example, some radical thinkers in the nineteenth century might embrace improvement in the sense of scientific farming, without its connotation of commercial profit. But in the early modern period, productivity and profit were inextricably connected in the concept of improvement, and it nicely sums up the ideology of a rising agrarian capitalism.

In the seventeenth century a whole new body of literature emerged, spelling out in unprecedented detail the techniques and benefits of improvement. Improvement was also a major preoccupation of the Royal Society, which brought together some of England's most prominent scientists (Isaac Newton and Robert Boyle were both members of the Society) with some of the more forward-looking members of England's ruling classes—like the first Earl of Shaftesbury, mentor of the philosopher John Locke, and Locke himself, both of whom were keenly interested in agricultural improvement.

Improvement did not, in the first instance, depend on significant technological innovations—although new equipment was used, like the wheel-plow. In general, it was more a matter of new developments in farming techniques or even just refinements and elaborations of old ones: "convertible" or "up and down" husbandry, alternating cultivation with fallow periods; crop rotation; drainage of marsh and plowlands; and so on.

But improvement meant something more than new or better methods and techniques of farming. Improvement meant, even more fundamentally, new forms and conceptions of property. For the enterprising landlord and his prosperous capitalist tenant, "improved" farming ideally though not necessarily meant enlarged and concentrated landholdings. It certainly meant the elimination of old customs and practices that interfered with the most productive use of land.

Peasants have since time immemorial employed various means of regulating land use in the interests of the village community. They have restricted certain practices and granted certain rights, not in order to enhance the wealth of landlords or states but in order to preserve the peasant community itself, perhaps to conserve the land or to distribute its fruits more equitably, and often to provide for the community's less fortunate members. Even private ownership of property has been typically conditioned by such customary practices, giving non-owners certain use rights to property owned by someone else. In England, there were many such practices and customs. There existed common lands, on which members of the community might have grazing rights or the right to collect firewood, and there were various other kinds of use rights on private land, such as the right to collect the leavings of the harvest during specified periods of the year.

From the standpoint of improving landlords and capitalist farmers, land had to be liberated from any such obstruction to their productive and profitable use of property. Between the sixteenth and eighteenth centuries, there was growing pressure to extinguish customary rights that interfered with capitalist accumulation. This could mean various things: disputing communal rights to common lands by claiming exclusive private ownership; eliminating various use rights on private land; or challenging the customary tenures that gave many smallholders rights of possession without unambiguous legal title. In all these cases, traditional conceptions of property had to be replaced by new, capitalist conceptions of property had to be replaced by new, capitalist conceptions of property—not only as "private" but as *exclusive*. Other individuals and the community had to be excluded by eliminating village regulation and restrictions on land use (something that did not, for example, happen in France in anything like the same ways and degrees), by extinguishing customary use rights, and so on.[6]

Enclosure

This brings us to the most famous redefinition of property rights: enclosure. Enclosure is often thought of as simply the fencing in of common land, or of the "open fields" that characterized certain parts of the English countryside. But enclosure meant the extinction, with or without a physical fencing of land, of common and customary use rights on which many people depended for their livelihood.

The first major wave of enclosure occurred in the sixteenth century, when larger landowners sought to drive commoners off lands that could be profitably put to use as pasture for increasingly lucrative sheep farming. Contemporary commentators held enclosure, more than any other single factor, responsible for the growing plague of vagabonds, those dispossessed "masterless men" who wandered the countryside and threatened social order.[7] The most famous of these commentators, Thomas More, though himself an encloser, described the practice as "sheep devouring men." These social critics, like many historians after them, may have overestimated the effects of enclosure at the expense of other factors leading to the transformation of English property relations. But it remains the most vivid expression of the relentless process that was changing not only the English countryside but the world: the birth of capitalism.

Enclosure continued to be a major source of conflict in early modern England, whether for sheep or increasingly profitable arable farming. Enclosure riots punctuated the sixteenth and seventeenth centuries, and enclosure surfaced as a major grievance in the English Civil War. In its earlier phases, the practice was to some degree resisted by the monarchical state, if only because of the threat to public order. But once the landed classes had succeeded in shaping the state to their own changing requirements—a success more or less finally consolidated in 1688, in the so-called Glorious Revolution—there was no further state interference, and a new kind of enclosure movement emerged in the eighteenth century, the so-called Parliamentary enclosures. In this kind of enclosure, the extinction of troublesome property rights that interfered with some landlord's powers of accumulation took place by acts of Parliament. Nothing more neatly testifies to the triumph of agrarian capitalism.

Locke's Theory of Property

The pressures to transform the nature of property manifested themselves in various ways, in theory and in practice. They surfaced in court cases, in conflicts over specific property rights, over some piece of common land or some private land to which different people had overlapping use rights. In such cases, customary practices and claims often directly confronted the principles of "improvement"—and judges often recognized reasons of improvement as legitimate claims against customary rights that had been in place as long as anyone could remember.[8] New conceptions of property were also being theorized more systematically, most famously in Chapter Five of John Locke's *Second Treatise of Government*, written in the late seventeenth century.[9] It is worth looking more closely at his argument, because there is no other work more emblematic of a rising agrarian capitalism.

Locke begins with the proposition that God "hath given the world to men in common" (II.26), but he goes on to show how, nevertheless, individuals came to have property in particular things. In fact, he writes, such private, individual property is a God-given natural right. Men (and in his argument, it is always men) own their own persons, and the labor that they do with their hands and bodies is therefore their property too. So, he argues, a natural right of property is established when a man "mixes his labor" with something, when, that is, by means of his labor he removes it from its natural state or changes its natural condition.

Locke's whole argument on property turns on the notion of "improvement." The theme running throughout the chapter is that the earth is there to be made productive and profitable, and that this is why private property, which emanates from labor, trumps common possession. Locke repeatedly insists that most of the value inherent in land comes not from nature but from labor and improvement: "'tis *labour* indeed that *puts the difference of value* on everything." (II.40) He even offers specific calculations of value contributed by labor as against nature. "I think," he suggests, for example, "it will be but a very modest Computation to say, that of the *Products* of the Earth useful to the Life of Man, 9/10 are the *effects of labour*," and then immediately corrects himself: it would be more accurate to say that 99/100 should be attributed to labor rather than to nature. (II.40) An acre of land in unimproved America, which may be as naturally fertile as an acre in England, is not worth 1/1000 of the English acre, if we calculate "all the Profit an *Indian* received from it." (II.43) Locke's point, which not coincidentally drips with colonialist contempt, is that unimproved land is *waste*, so that any man who takes it out of common ownership and appropriates it to himself—he who removes land from the common and encloses it—in order to improve it has *given* something to humanity, not taken it away.

There is, of course, something attractive about Locke's idea that labor is the source of value and the basis of property, but it soon becomes clear that there is something odd about it too. For one thing, it turns out that there is no direct correspondence between labor and property, because one man can appropriate the labor of another. He can acquire a right of property in something by "mixing" with it not his own labor but the labor of someone else whom he employs. It appears that the issue for Locke has less to do with the activity of labor as such than with its profitable use. In calculating the value of the acre in America, for instance, he does not talk about the Indian's expenditure of effort, labor, but about the Indian's failure to realize a profit. The issue, in other words, is not the labor of a human being but the *productivity of property* and its application to commercial profit.

In a famous and much debated passage, Locke writes that "the Grass my Horse has bit; the Turfs my Servant has cut; and the Ore I have digg'd in any place where I have a right to them in common with others, become my *Property*. . . ." (II.28) Much ink has been spilled on this passage and what it tells us about, for example, Locke's views on wage labor (the labor of the servant who cuts the turfs). But what is truly striking about the passage is that Locke treats "the Turfs my Servant has cut" as equivalent to "the Ore I have digg'd." This means not only that I, the master, have appropriated the labor of my servant, but that this appropriation is in principle no different from the servant's laboring activity itself. My own digging is, for all intents and purposes, the same as my appropriating the fruits of my servant's cutting. But Locke is not interested in simply *passive* appropriation. The point is rather that the landlord who puts his land to productive use, who improves it, even if it is by means of someone else's labor, is being *industrious,* no less—and perhaps more—than the laboring servant.

This is a point worth dwelling on. One way of understanding what Locke is driving at is to consider common usage today. When the financial pages of the daily newspaper speak of "producers," they do not normally mean *workers.* In fact, they are likely to talk about conflicts, for example, between automobile "producers" and auto workers or their unions. The employers of labor, in other words, are being credited with "production." We have become so accustomed to this usage that we fail to see its implications, but it is important to keep in mind that certain very specific historical conditions were required to make it possible.

Traditional ruling classes in a pre-capitalist society, passively appropriating rents from dependent peasants, would never think of themselves as "producers." The kind of appropriation that can be called "productive" is distinctively capitalist. It implies that property is used *actively*, not for conspicuous consumption but for investment and increasing profit. Wealth is acquired not simply by using coercive force to extract more surplus labor from direct producers, in the manner of rentier aristocrats, nor by buying cheap and selling dear like pre-capitalist merchants, but by increasing labor productivity (output per unit of work).

By conflating labor with the production of profit, Locke becomes perhaps the first thinker to construct a systematic theory of property based on something like these capitalist principles. He is certainly not a theorist of a mature, industrial capitalism. But his view of property, with its emphasis on productivity, already sets him apart from his predecessors. His idea that value is actively created in production is already vastly different from traditional views which focus simply on the process of exchange, the "sphere of circulation." Only William Petty, often called the founder of political economy, had suggested anything like this "labor theory of value" in the seventeenth century, and that too in the context of agrarian capitalism—a theory he tested as an imperial agent in Ireland, just as Locke and his mentor the first Earl of Shaftesbury looked upon the American colonies as a laboratory of improvement.[10]

Locke in his economic works is critical of those landed aristocrats who sit back and collect rents without improving their land, and he is equally critical of merchants who simply act as middlemen, buying cheap in one market and selling at a higher price in another, or hoarding goods to raise their price, or cornering a market to increase the profits of sale. Both types of proprietor are, in his view, parasitic. Yet his attack on proprietors of this kind should not be misread as a defense of working people against the dominant classes. He certainly has good things to say about industrious artisans and tradesmen, but his ideal seems to be the great improving landlord, whom he regards as the ultimate source of wealth in the community, what he calls, significantly, the "first producer"—a man like Shaftesbury, capitalist landlord and investor in colonial trade, a man who is not only "industrious" but whose vast property contributes greatly to the wealth of the community.

Locke's view of property is very well suited to the conditions of England in the early days of agrarian capitalism. It clearly reflects a condition in which highly concentrated landownership and large holdings were associated with a uniquely productive agri-culture (again, productive not just in the sense of total output but output per unit of work). His language of improvement echoes the scientific literature devoted to the techniques of agriculture which flourished uniquely in England at this time—especially emanating from the Royal Society and the groups of learned men with whom Locke and Shaftesbury were closely connected. More particularly, his constant references to common land as *waste* and his praise for the removal of land from the common, and indeed for enclosure, had very powerful resonances in that time and place.

We need to be reminded that the definition of property was in Locke's day not just a philosophical issue but a very immediate practical one. As we have seen, a new, capitalist definition of property was in the process of establishing itself, challenging traditional forms not just in theory but in practice. The idea of overlapping use rights to the same piece of land was giving way in England to *exclusive* ownership. From the sixteenth to the eighteenth century, there were constant disputes over common and customary rights. Increasingly, the principle of improvement for profitable exchange was taking precedence over other prin-ciples and other claims to property, whether those claims were based on custom or on some fundamental right of subsistence.

Enhancing productivity itself became a reason for excluding other rights.

What better argument than Locke's could be found to support the landlord seeking to extinguish the customary rights of commoners, to exclude them from common land, and to turn common land into exclusive private property by means of enclosure? What better argument than that enclosure, exclusion, and improvement enhanced the wealth of the community and added more to the "common stock" than it subtracted? And indeed, there were in the seventeenth century already examples of legal decisions in conflicts over land where judges invoked principles very much like those outlined by Locke, in order to give exclusive property precedence over common and customary rights. In the eighteenth century, when enclosure would accelerate rapidly with the active involvement of Parliament, reasons of "improvement" would be cited systematically as the basis of title to property and as grounds for extinguishing traditional rights.

This is not the only way in which Locke's theory of property supported the interests of landlords like Shaftesbury. Against the background of his emphatic pronouncement that all men were free and equal in the state of nature, he found ingenious ways of justifying slavery. And his views on improvement could easily be mobilized to justify colonial expansion and the expropriation of indigenous peoples, as his remark on the American Indian makes painfully obvious. If the unimproved lands of the Americas represented nothing but "waste," it was a divinely ordained duty for Europeans to enclose and improve them, just as "industrious" and "rational" men had done in the original state of nature. "In the beginning all the World was *America*" (II.49), with no money, no commerce, no improvement. If the world—or some of it—had been removed from that natural state at the behest of God, anything that remained in such a primitive condition must surely go the same way.

Class Struggle

It should be clear at this point that the development of distinctive property forms in English agriculture entailed new forms of class struggle. Here again, we can highlight the specificity of agrarian capitalism by contrasting the English situation to the French. The differences in property forms and modes of exploitation which, as we have seen, characterized these two major European powers were reflected in different issues and terrains of class struggle, and different relations between class and state.

In France, extra-economic modes of surplus extraction or politically constituted property, whether in the form of state office or the various powers and privileges attached to noble status (such as exemptions from taxes), set the terms of class struggle. The state, for instance, served as a source of income for a substantial segment of the dominant classes. At the same time, the state, as a form of politically constituted property, competed with landed classes for the same peasant-produced surpluses. So parts of the aristocracy might struggle against the efforts of the monarchy to suppress their autonomous powers and appropriate them to a centralized absolutist state, while others held or sought to acquire property in that very state. A bourgeois might oppose the excessive burden of taxation borne by the unprivileged Third Estate and the exemptions enjoyed by the privileged estates, the nobility and the church, while at the same time he might seek state office (which could be bought) as a means of appropriating surplus labor through taxation. Peasants were, of course, the primary source of that surplus labor, which meant that as the state and its apparatus of offices grew and peasants were subject to an ever-increasing burden of taxation, the peasantry had to be preserved by the monarchy from destruction by rent-hungry landlords in order to be squeezed by a tax-hungry state.

Appropriating classes, then, had a material interest in preserving or obtaining access to politically constituted property, whether in the form of privilege or directly in state office. This would prove a major issue in the Revolution of 1789, when aristocratic privilege was challenged by the Third Estate, and when the bourgeoisie in particular reacted against the threat to close their access to state office.[11] For producing classes, and peasants in particular, the single largest class issue throughout the *ancien regime* was undoubtedly the burden of taxation, and popular resistance was likely to focus above all on exploitation by the state in the form of steeply rising taxes.

The picture was very different in early modern England. There, politically constituted property was not a major issue. The landed class, in its growing reliance on purely economic forms of exploitation, never relied so much on the state as a direct material resource, and royal taxation never played the same role for the English propertied classes as it did for the French. While English landlords relied on the state to enforce their class interests—and would come into conflict with it when their property, or the powers of Parliament as a committee of propertyholders, were challenged by the monarchy—their direct material interests lay not in acquiring a piece of the state so much as in enhancing their *economic* powers of appropriation, the powers rooted directly in their control of land and its productive uses. While the French aristocrat might be preoccupied with retaining his access to high office or his tax exemptions and various noble privileges, the right of enclosure might figure more prominently on the class agenda of the English landlord.

For subordinate classes in England, this meant that conflicts over property rights, over the very *meaning* of property, loomed larger than struggles against extra-economic exploitation. So, for instance, resistance to enclosure, or the protection of customary use rights, would, for the English commoner, occupy the prominent position in struggles against exploitation that resistance to taxation did for the French peasant.

This also raises some important questions about the role of class struggle in the development of capitalism. What, for instance, can we say now about the argument that class struggle by peasants against landlords promoted capitalism in England by throwing off the shackles of feudalism and liberating commodity production? While the configuration of class relations was too complex to be reduced to any simple formula, if we want to sum up in a single sentence the ways in which class struggle between landlords and peasants "liberated" capitalism, it might be closer to the truth to say that capitalism was advanced by the assertion of the landlords' powers against the peasants' claims to customary rights. This is not, again, to dismiss the role of "middling" farmers, or the English yeoman, in the development of capitalism. These farmers, as capitalist tenants, were the backbone of the agrarian triad. But it is surely misleading to treat popular struggles as the major force in advancing the development of capitalism at the expense of more subversive and democratic popular struggles which *challenged* property forms conducive to capitalist development. These popular forces may have lost the battle against capitalist landlords, but they left a tremendous legacy of radical ideas quite distinct from the "progressive" impulses of capitalism, a legacy that is still alive today in various democratic and anti-capitalist movements.[12]

The situation is even more complicated when it comes to "bourgeois revolution." The French Revolution of 1789 fits the description far better than the English Revolution of the 1640s—if what we are looking for is a major struggle between bourgeoisie and aristocracy. But, as we have seen, there are some very large questions about what the struggle in France had to do with capitalism. The English Revolution, by contrast, was certainly not a conflict between bourgeoisie and aristocracy. But by enhancing the power of the propertied classes in Parliament and by advancing the interests of larger against smaller landowners, and "improvement" against the customary rights of subordinate classes, it had more to do, and more directly, with the promotion of capitalism and the capitalist definition of property than did the Revolution in France.

Chapter Five

From Agrarian to Industrial Capitalism: A Brief Sketch

IN ENGLAND, WHERE WEALTH STILL DERIVED PREDOMINANTLY from agricultural production, all major economic actors in the agrarian sector—both direct producers and the appropriators of their surpluses—were, from the sixteenth century, increasingly dependent on what amounted to capitalist practices: the maximization of exchange value by means of cost-cutting and improving productivity, through specialization, accumulation, and innovation.

This mode of providing for the basic material needs of English society brought with it a whole new dynamic of self-sustaining growth, a process of accumulation and expansion very different from the age-old cyclical patterns that dominated material life in other societies. It was also accompanied by the typical capitalist processes of expropriation and the creation of a propertyless mass. It is in this sense that we can speak of "agrarian capitalism" in early modern England, a social form with distinctive "laws of motion" which would eventually give rise to capitalism in its mature, industrial form. It is not the purpose of this book to explore the whole history of capitalist development, but we can at least sketch out some of the connections between capitalism in its original agrarian form and its later industrial development.

Was Agrarian Capitalism Really Capitalist?

We should pause here to emphasize two major points. First, it was not merchants or manufacturers who were driving the process that propelled the early development of capitalism. The transformation of social property relations was firmly rooted in the countryside, and the transformation of English trade and industry was result more than cause of England's transition to capitalism. Merchants could function perfectly well within non-capitalist systems. They prospered, for example, in the context of European feudalism, where they profited not only from the autonomy of cities but also from the fragmentation of markets and the opportunity to conduct transactions between one market and another.

Secondly, and even more fundamentally, the term "agrarian capitalism" has so far been used without placing wage labor at its core, although by any definition wage labor is central to capitalism. This requires some explanation.

It should be said that many tenants did employ wage labor, so much so that the triad identified by Marx and others—landlords living on capitalist ground rent, capitalist tenants living on profit, and laborers living on wages—has been regarded by many as the defining characteristic of agrarian relations in England. And so it was, at least in those parts of the country, particularly the east and southeast, most noted for their agricultural productivity. In fact, the new economic pressures, the competitive pressures that drove unproductive farmers to the wall, were a major factor in polarizing the agrarian population into larger landholders and propertyless wage laborers, promoting the agrarian triad. And, of course, the pressures to increase productivity made themselves felt in the intensified exploitation of wage labor.

It would not, then, be unreasonable to define English agrarian capitalism in terms of the triad. But it is important to keep in mind that competitive pressures, and the new "laws of motion" that went with them, depended in the first instance not on the existence of a mass proletariat but on the existence of market-dependent tenant-producers. Wage laborers, and especially those who depended entirely on wages for their livelihood and not just for seasonal supplements (the kind of seasonal and supplementary wage labor that has existed since ancient times in peasant societies) remained very much a minority in seventeenth-century England.

Besides, these competitive pressures affected not just tenants who employed wage laborers but also farmers who—typically with their families—were themselves direct producers working without hired labor. People could be market-dependent—dependent on the market for the basic conditions of their self-reproduction—without being completely dispossessed. To be market-dependent required only the loss of direct non-market access to the means of self-reproduction. In fact, once market imperatives were well-established, even outright ownership was no protection against them. And market dependence was a cause, not a result, of mass proletarianization.

In other words, the specific dynamics of capitalism were already in place in English agriculture before the proletarianization of the work force. In fact, those dynamics were a major factor in bringing about the proletarianization of labor in England. The critical factor was the market dependence of producers, as well as appropriators, and the new social imperatives created by that market dependence.

Some people may be reluctant to describe this social formation as "capitalist" on the grounds that capitalism is, by definition, based on the exploitation of wage labor. That reluctance is fair enough—as long as we recognize that, whatever we call it, the English economy in the early modern period, driven by the logic of its basic productive sector, agriculture, was already operating according to principles and "laws of motion" different from those prevailing in any other society since the dawn of history. Those laws of motion were the *preconditions*—which existed nowhere else—for the development of a mature capitalism that would indeed be based on the mass exploitation of wage labor.

What, then, was the outcome of all this? First, English agriculture was uniquely productive. By the end of the seventeenth century, for instance, grain and cereal production had risen so dramatically that England became a leading exporter of those commodities. These advances in production were achieved with a relatively small agricultural labor force. This is what it means to speak of the unique *productivity* of English agriculture.

Some historians have, as we have seen, tried to challenge the very idea of agrarian capitalism by suggesting that the "productivity" of French agriculture in the eighteenth century was more or less equal to that of England. What they really mean is that *total agricultural production* in the two countries was more or less equal. But in one country that level of production was achieved by a population the vast majority of which still consisted of peasant producers, while in the other country the same total production was achieved by a much smaller work force, in a declining rural population. The issue, again, is not total output but *productivity*, output per unit of work.

The demographic facts alone speak volumes. It is not uncommon to acknowledge that England's agricultural productivity was uniquely capable of sustaining a population explosion that helped to fuel industrialization. But by the time England's population density began to eclipse that of other countries in Western Europe, when their population growth had leveled off if not declined, the pattern of English economic development was already distinctive.

A demographic increase may help to explain the development of industrial capitalism, but it cannot explain the emergence of capitalism itself. If anything, that population explosion was effect rather than cause. But even before a unique pattern of population increase became manifest in England, its demographic composition was already distinct in other significant ways, which tell us a great deal about English economic development.

Between 1500 and 1700, when England experienced a substantial growth in population like that of other European countries, English population growth was distinctive in one major respect: the percentage of its urban population more than doubled in that period (some historians put the urban percentage at just under a quarter of the total population already by the late seventeenth century). The contrast with France is telling. There, the rural population remained fairly stable, still about 85 to 90 percent at the time of the French Revolution in 1789 and beyond. By 1850, when the urban population of England and Wales was about 40.8 per cent, France's was still only 14.4 per cent (and Germany's 10.8).[1]

So already in the early modern period, British agriculture was productive enough to sustain an unusually large number of people no longer engaged in agricultural production. This fact, of course, testifies to more than just particularly efficient farming techniques. It also bespeaks a revolution in social property relations. While France remained a country of peasant proprietors, land in England was concentrated in far fewer hands, and the propertyless mass was growing rapidly. The central issue, however, is not the size of holdings. While agricultural production in France still followed traditional peasant practices (nothing like the English body of improvement literature existed in France, and the village community still imposed its regulations and restrictions on production, even affecting larger landholders), English farming was responding to the imperatives of competition and improvement.[2]

It is worth adding one other point about England's distinctive demographic pattern. The unusual growth of the urban population was not evenly distributed among English towns. Elsewhere in Europe, the typical pattern was an urban population scattered among several important towns—so that, for example, Lyons was not dwarfed by Paris. In England, London became disproportionately huge, growing from about 60,000 inhabitants around 1530 to 575,000 in 1700 and becoming the largest city in Europe, while other English towns were much smaller.

This pattern signifies more than is apparent at first glance. It testifies, among other things, to the transformation of social property relations in the heartland of agrarian capitalism, the south and southeast, and the dispossession of small producers, whose destination as displaced migrants would typically be London. The growth of London also represents the growing unification not only of the English state but of a national market. That huge city was the hub of English commerce. It was both a major transit point for national and international trade and a vast consumer of English products, not least its agricultural produce. The growth of London, in other words, in all kinds of ways stands for England's emerging capitalism: its increasingly single, unified, integrated, and competitive market; its productive agriculture; and its dispossessed population.

Commerce, Empire, and Industry

The distinctive and unprecedented logic of agrarian capitalism made itself felt in every sphere of economic life. It is certainly true that English capitalism emerged in the context of a larger trading system and would not have emerged without that. But contrary to conventions that find the driving force of economic development in commercial activity, the economic "laws of motion" born in the English countryside transformed the age-old rules of trade and created an entirely new kind of commercial system. That system depended not only on foreign trade, the kind of carrying trade described by Polanyi, but on a highly developed domestic market, with a growing population no longer engaged in producing everyday goods—like food and textiles—for their own and their families' consumption. London itself was a massive market for basic consumer goods, and it was the hub of this growing domestic market, a market that differed from others in size, substance, and "laws of motion."

This was the first, and for a long time the only, commercial system based on trade in the means of survival and self-reproduction for a growing mass market, not luxury goods for a limited market.[3] The increasingly national, integrated nature of that market meant that it was increasingly operating not simply on the principles of "profit on alienation" but on the basis of competitive production.

England even developed its own distinctive banking system. Other major European trading centers had banking systems that had evolved in ancient and medieval times: moneychanging operations, public banks dealing with state finances and currency regulation, and mechanisms for financing foreign and long-distance trade. England was relatively weak in banking of this "classical" kind, but it created a new banking system that originated, in contrast to the rest of Europe, in domestic trade, largely in domestic products. This system was not rooted in foreign trade, "not in commercial arbitrage between separate markets," but in a "metropolitan market" centered on London, to facilitate a network of distribution from London outwards throughout the country, by means of "factors" or agents who operated on commissions and credits.[4] It is not difficult to see that this distinctive financial and commercial system had its roots in agrarian capitalism, in the changing social relations that produced both a need for such a market to sustain a growing non-agrarian population and the capacity to meet that need.

The dynamics of the English domestic market expanded outward into international trade. The developing national economy was also becoming the center of an international commercial system different from any trading system before it. Just as the old network of local markets and the "carrying" trade between them were giving way to an integrated market, a system of world commerce originating in Britain, and especially in London, was emerging which would replace "the infinite succession of arbitrage operations between separate, distinct, and discrete markets that had previously constituted foreign trade."[5] The characteristic instruments produced by the English domestic commercial system, bills of exchange and especially the "bills on London," also became the instruments of international trade. When England gained unambiguous ascendancy in international commerce, in what is sometimes called the "commercial capitalism" of the eighteenth century, its success was built on the foundations of the earlier domestic commercial system—and even the military power, the massive naval power, that secured British pre-eminence was clearly rooted in the wealth created by agrarian capitalism.

The new dynamics of this growing capitalist system produced a new form of colonial imperialism. There had been other, even larger and more powerful, colonial states. But Britain created a new kind of imperial drive: not just the age-old pre-capitalist hunger for land and plunder (though that, of course, did not disappear) but an outward expansion of the same capitalist imperatives that were driving the domestic market, the imperatives of competitive production and expanding consumption.

As early as the seventeenth century, or perhaps even the sixteenth, the distinctive attitudes and behavior of English imperialists were visible in England's first major colony, Ireland. Forward-looking public servants, like the political economist William Petty, saw Ireland as a testing ground for agrarian capitalism, a laboratory in which to test the effects of transforming property relations, whatever the consequences for the multitudes of dispossessed.

British imperialism also, of course, contributed to the development of the world's first industrial capitalism. But while industrialization did feed on the resources of empire, it is important to keep in mind that the logic of imperialism did not bring about industrial capitalism by itself. Imperial power in other European states did not produce the same effects, and on the eve of the Industrial Revolution, the domestic market was still more important in the British economy than was international trade. Agrarian capitalism was the root of British economic development.

Marxist historians have persuasively demonstrated, against many arguments to the contrary, that the greatest crime of European empire, slavery, made a major contribution to the development of industrial capitalism.[6] But here, too, we have to keep in mind that Britain was not alone in exploiting colonial slavery and that elsewhere it had different effects. Other major European powers—France, Spain, Portugal—amassed great wealth from slavery and from the trade in addictive goods like tobacco which, it has been argued, fueled the trade in living human beings.[7] But, again, only in Britain was that wealth converted into industrial capital—and here again the difference lies in the new capitalist dynamic which had already transformed the logic of the British economy, setting in train the imperatives of competitive production, capital accumulation, and self-sustaining growth.

Trade and empire, then, were essential factors in the development of industrial capitalism, but they cannot be treated as primary causes. To put it another way, their specific effects varied greatly according to their context. We have to look to the English domestic market, and to the agrarian capitalism in which it grew, to find the *differentia specifica* that harnessed commerce and empire to capitalist industry.

The long-term consequences of England's agrarian capitalism for subsequent economic development should be fairly obvious.

Although this is not the place to explore in detail the connections between agrarian capitalism and England's development into the first "industrialized" economy, some points are self-evident. Without a productive agricultural sector which could sustain a large non-agricultural workforce, the world's first industrial capitalism would have been unlikely to emerge. Without England's agrarian capitalism, there would have been no dispossessed mass obliged to sell its labor power for a wage. Without that dispossessed non-agrarian work force, there would have been no mass consumer market for the cheap everyday goods—such as food and textiles—that drove the process of industrialization in England. It is worth emphasizing that this large market derived its special character not only from its unusual size but also from its limitations, the relative poverty of consumers demanding cheap goods for everyday use. It had more in common with later mass consumer markets than with the luxury trade of "classical" commerce.

Without the wealth created by agrarian capitalism, together with wholly new motivations for colonial expansion—motivations different from the old forms of territorial acquisition—British imperialism would have been a very different thing than the engine of industrial capitalism it was to become. Finally (this is no doubt a more contentious point) without English capitalism there would probably have been no capitalist system of any kind: it was competitive pressures emanating from England, especially an industrialized England, that, in the first instance, compelled other countries to promote their own economic development in capitalist directions. States still acting on pre-capitalist principles of trade, or geo-political and military rivalry hardly different in principle from older, feudal conflicts over territory and plunder, would be driven by England's new competitive advantages to promote their own economic development in similar ways.[8]

At the very least, agrarian capitalism made industrialization possible. To say even this is already to say a great deal. The conditions of possibility created by agrarian capitalism—the transformations in property relations, in the size and nature of the domestic market, the composition of the population, and in the nature and extent of British trade and British imperialism—were more substantial and far-reaching than any purely technological advances required by industrialization. This is true in two senses: first, purely technological advances, again, were not responsible for the so-called agricultural revolution that laid the foundation of industrialization; and second, the technological changes that constituted the first "Industrial Revolution" were in any case modest.[9]

Whether agrarian capitalism made industrial capitalism not only possible but necessary or inevitable is another question, but there was a strong historical impulse in that direction. An integrated market providing cheap necessities of life for a growing mass of consumers and responding to already well-established competitive pressures constituted a new and specific "logic of process," the outcome of which was industrial capitalism. That market, and the social property relations in which it was rooted, provided not only the means but the need to produce consumer goods on a new scale, and also to produce them cost-effectively, in ways determined by the imperatives of competition, accumulation, and profit maximization, together with their requirements for improving labor productivity.

In other words, in contrast to Polanyi's suggestion that "market society" was a response to certain technological developments in a commercial society, the conclusion we can draw from the history of agrarian capitalism is that a capitalist dynamic rooted in a new form of social property relations preceded industrialization, both chronologically and causally. In fact, a kind of market society—a society in which producers were dependent on the market for access to the means of life, labor, and self-reproduction, and subject to market imperatives—was not the *result* of industrialization but its primary cause. Only a transformation in social property relations that compelled people to produce competitively (and not just to buy cheap and sell dear), a transformation that made access to the means of self-reproduction dependent on the market, can explain the dramatic revolutionizing of productive forces uniquely characteristic of modern capitalism.

Industrialization was, then, the result not the cause of market society, and capitalist laws of motion were the cause not the result of mass proletarianization. But that, of course, was not the end of capitalist development. Proletarianization, which meant the complete commodification of labor power, would confer new and more far-reaching coercive powers on the market by creating a working class that was completely market-dependent and completely vulnerable to market disciplines, with no mediations and no alternative resources. While both capital and labor were in their various ways subject to the impersonal forces of the market, the market itself would become increasingly a major axis of class division between exploiters and exploited, between buyers and sellers of labor power. In that sense, it was a new coercive instrument for capital, the ultimate discipline in its control of labor, and a new terrain of class struggle.

The capitalist system is, needless to say, in a constant state of development and flux. But we will not understand its current processes of change and contradiction if we fail to trace them to their foundations. The rise of capitalism cannot be explained as the outcome of technical improvements, "the Western European trend of economic progress," or any other transhistorical mechanism. The specific transformation of social property relations that *set in train* a historically unique "progress" of productive forces cannot be taken for granted. To acknowledge this is critical to an understanding of capitalism—not to mention the conditions of its abolition and replacement by a different social form. We must recognize not only the full force of capitalist imperatives, the compulsions of accumulation, profit maximization, and increasing labor productivity, but also their systemic roots, so we know just why they work the way they do.

Chapter Six

Modernity and Postmodernity

THE NATURALIZATION OF CAPITALISM IMPLICIT IN THE conventional identification of *bourgeois* with *capitalist* and both with *modernity,* which still persists even in today's most iconoclastic theories, has the effect of disguising the specificity of capitalism, if not conceptualizing it away altogether. Now let us turn briefly to the other side of the coin. The point is not just that capitalism is historically specific. It is that if some essential aspects of "modernity" have little to do with capitalism, then the identification of capitalism with modernity may disguise the specificity of a *non*-capitalist modernity, too.

Modernity versus Capitalism: France and England

Whatever else people mean by "modernity," and whether they think it is good or bad or both, they usually believe it has something to do with what sociologist Max Weber called the process of *rationalization:* the rationalization of the state in bureaucratic organization, the rationalization of the economy in industrial capitalism, the rationalization of culture in the spread of education, the decline of superstition, and the progress of science and technology, and so on. The process of rationalization is typically associated with certain intellectual or cultural patterns that go back to the Enlightenment: rationalism and an obsession with rational planning, a fondness for "totalizing" views of the world, the standardization of knowledge, universalism (a belief in universal truths and values), and a belief in linear progress, especially of reason and freedom.

The Enlightenment is typically conceived of as a, if not *the*, major turning point in the advance of modernity, and the conflation of modernity with capitalism is most readily visible in the way theories of modernity connect the Enlightenment with capitalism. The characteristic features of the Enlightenment are supposed to be associated with the development of capitalism, either because early capitalism, in the process of unfolding itself, created them, or because the advancement of "rationalization" that produced the Enlightenment also brought capitalism with it. Weber, for instance, is famous for distinguishing among various meanings of rationality (formal or instrumental versus substantive, and so on), yet his argument about the historical process of rationalization depends, of course, on *assimilating* the various meanings of reason and rationality, so that the instrumental rationality of capitalism is by definition related to reason in its Enlightenment meaning. For better or worse, the process that brought us the best of Enlightenment principles—a resistance to all arbitrary power, a commitment to universal human emancipation, and a critical stance toward all kinds of authority, whether intellectual, religious, or political—is, according to this view, the same process that brought us the capitalist organization of production.

To unravel the conflation of capitalism and modernity, we might begin by situating the Enlightenment in its own historical setting. Much of the Enlightenment project belongs to a distinctly *non*-capitalist society—not just *pre*-capitalist but non-capitalist. Many features of the Enlightenment, in other words, are rooted in non-capitalist social property relations. They belong to a social form that is not just a transitional point on the way to capitalism but an alternative route out of feudalism. In particular, the French Enlightenment belongs to the absolutist state in France.

The absolutist state in eighteenth-century France, as we saw in the discussion of Anderson, functioned not just as a political form but as an economic resource for a substantial section of the ruling class. In that sense, it represents not just the political but the economic or material context of the Enlightenment. The absolutist state was a centralized instrument of extra-economic surplus extraction, and office in the state was a form of property which gave its possessors access to peasant-produced surpluses. There also were other, decentralized forms of extra-economic appropriation, the residues of feudalism and its so-called parcellized sovereignties. These forms of extra-economic appropriation were, in other words, directly antithetical to the purely *economic* form of *capitalist* exploitation.

Now consider the fact that the principal home of the so-called project of modernity, eighteenth-century France, was an overwhelmingly rural society, with a limited and fragmented internal market. Its market still operated on non-capitalist principles: not the appropriation of surplus value from commodified labor power, not the creation of value in production, but the age-old practices of commercial profit-taking—profit on alienation, buying cheap and selling dear, trading typically in luxury goods or supplies for the state. The overwhelmingly peasant population was the antithesis of a mass consumer market. As for the bourgeoisie which is supposed to be the main material source, so to speak, of the Enlightenment, it was *not* a capitalist class. In fact, it was not, for the most part, even a traditional commercial class. The main bourgeois actors in the Enlightenment, and later in the French Revolution, were professionals, officeholders, and intellectuals. Their quarrel with the aristocracy had little to do with liberating capitalism from the fetters of feudalism.

Where, then, did the principles of so-called modernity come from? Did they come out of a new but growing capitalism? Did they represent an aspiring capitalist class struggling against a feudal aristocracy? Can we at least say that capitalism was the unintended consequence of the project of bourgeois modernity? Or did that project represent something different?

Consider the class interests of the French bourgeoisie. One way of focusing on them is to turn to the French Revolution, the culmination of the Enlightenment project. What were the main revolutionary objectives of the bourgeoisie? At the core of its program were civil equality, the attack on privilege, and a demand for "careers open to talent." This meant, for example, equal access to the highest state offices, which the aristocracy tended to monopolize and which they were threatening to close off altogether. It also meant a more equitable system of taxation, so that the burden would no longer be disproportionately carried by the Third Estate for the benefit of the privileged estates, among whose most cherished privileges were exemptions from taxation. The main targets of these complaints were the aristocracy and, secondarily, the Church.

How did these bourgeois interests express themselves ideologically? Take the example of universalism, the belief in certain principles which apply to humanity in general at all times and places. Universalism has had a long history in the West, but it had a very special meaning and salience for the French bourgeoisie. To put it briefly, the bourgeois challenge to privilege and the privileged estates, to the nobility and the Church, expressed itself in asserting universalism against aristocratic particularism. The bourgeoisie challenged the aristocracy by invoking the universal principles of citizenship, civic equality, and the "nation"—a universalistic identity which transcended the more particular and exclusive identities of kinship, tribe, village, status, estate, or class.

In other words, *universality* was opposed to *privilege* in its literal meaning as a special or private law. Universality stood against differential privilege and prescriptive right. It was a fairly easy step from attacking traditional privilege to attacking the principles of custom and tradition in general. And this kind of challenge easily became a theory of history, in which the bourgeoisie and its organic intellectuals were assigned a leading role as the historic agents of a rupture with the past, the embodiments of reason and freedom, the vanguard of progress.

As for the bourgeois attitude toward the absolutist state, it is rather more ambiguous. As long as the bourgeoisie had reasonable access to lucrative state careers, the monarchical state suited it well, and even later, the so-called bourgeois revolution completed the centralizing project of absolutism. In fact, in some ways the bourgeois challenge to the traditional order, far from repudiating absolutist principles, simply extended them.

Take, again, the principle of universality. The monarchical state even in the sixteenth century had challenged the feudal claims of the nobility—often with the support of the Third Estate and the bourgeoisie in particular—by claiming to represent universality against the particularity of the nobility and other competing jurisdictions. The bourgeoisie also inherited and extended other absolutist principles: the preoccupation with rational planning and standardization, for example, something pioneered by the absolutist state and its leading officials, like Richelieu and Colbert. After all, even the standardization of the French language was part of the absolutist state's centralizing project, a project of "rationalization" that had its classic cultural expression in the formal gardens at Versailles.[1]

Scholars like Marshall Berman and David Harvey, who have given us some of the most important treatments of modernity (and postmodernity), like to emphasize the duality of the modern consciousness, which goes back to the Enlightenment. That dualistic sensibility, they say, combines universality and immutability with a sensitivity to ephemerality, contingency, fragmentation. The argument seems to be that the preoccupation with universality and absolute truth was from the start an attempt to make sense out of the fleeting, ephemeral, and constantly mobile and changing experience of modern life, which they associate with capitalism.

Berman quotes some passages from Rousseau's novel *Julie, ou La Nouvelle Héloïse* (1761), as one of the earliest expressions of that sensibility (he calls Rousseau "the archetypal modern voice in the early phase of modernity").[2] The most telling passage comes from a letter in which Rousseau's character St. Preux records his reactions on coming to Paris. What Berman sees here is the modern sense of new possibilities combined with the unease and uncertainty that comes from constant motion, change, and diversity. It is an experience that Berman associates with an early phase of capitalism.

But we can perhaps see something rather different in the words of St. Preux, or even in Berman's own account of the "maelstrom" of modern life. We can see not so much the experience of modern *capitalism* but the age-old fear and fascination aroused by the *city*. So much of what Rousseau's St. Preux, and Marshall Berman himself, have to say about the experience of "modern life" could have been said by the Italian countryman arriving in the ancient city of Rome. It may be significant that the Roman philosopher Seneca is a thinker for whom Rousseau himself expresses a special affinity, quoting him on the title page of *Émile* (1762) on a theme that is central to *La Nouvelle Héloïse,* and to Rousseau's work in general, the need to restore the health of humanity by a return to natural principles. For all Rousseau's so-called romanticism, the sensibility of the *La Nouvelle Héloïse* may indeed have more in common with ancient Stoicism than with the "experience of [capitalist] modernity." But in any case, it may be no accident that the literary tropes associated with this "experience of modernity"—Rousseau's and those of other European writers—typically come not from a highly urbanized society but from societies with a still overwhelmingly rural population.

At any rate, the ideology of the French bourgeoisie in the eighteenth century had not much to do with capitalism and much more to do with struggles over *non*-capitalist forms of appropriation, conflicts over extra-economic powers of exploitation. There is no need to reduce the Enlightenment to crude class ideology. The point is rather that in this particular historical conjuncture, in distinctly non-capitalist conditions, even bourgeois class ideology took the form of a larger vision of general human emancipation, not just emancipation for the bourgeoisie. For all its limitations, this was an emancipatory universalism—which is, of course, why it could be taken up by much more democratic and revolutionary forces.

To see the complexities here, we need only compare France with England. To reiterate, England in the eighteenth century at the height of agrarian capitalism had a growing urban population, which formed a much larger proportion of the total population than in France. Small proprietors were being dispossessed, not just by direct coercion but also by economic pressures. London was the largest city in Europe. There was a far more integrated— and competitive—internal market, the first national market in the world. There already existed the beginning of a mass consumer market for cheap everyday goods, especially food and textiles, and an increasingly proletarianized work force. England's productive base in agriculture was already operating on basically capitalist principles, with an aristocracy deeply involved in agrarian capitalism and new forms of commerce. And England was in the process of creating an industrial capitalism.

What were the characteristic cultural and ideological expressions of English capitalism in the same period?[3] Not Cartesian rationalism and rational planning but the "invisible hand" of classical political economy and the philosophy of British empiricism. Not the formal garden of Versailles but the irregular, apparently unplanned, "natural" landscape garden. Even the English state which promoted the early rise of capitalism was far less "rational" in Weberian terms than was the bureaucratic state of the French *ancien régime,* and the English legal system based on the common law is to this day less "rational" than the Napoleonic code that followed the French Revolution, or other continental systems based on Roman law. Certainly there was, in England, an interest in science and technology shared with its European neighbors. And after all, the French Enlightenment owed much to Bacon, Locke, and Newton. But the characteristic ideology that set England apart from other European cultures was above all the ideology of "improvement": not the Enlightenment idea of the improvement of humanity but the improvement of property, the ethic—and indeed the science—of profit, the commitment to increasing the productivity of labor, and the practice of enclosure and dispossession.

This ideology, especially the notion of agricultural improvement and the associated improvement literature produced in England, was not as characteristic of eighteenth-century France, where peasants dominated production and landlords retained their rentier mentality—as, for that matter, did the bourgeoisie on the whole. (The exception, by the way, proves the rule: the Physiocrats, those French political economists for whom *English* agriculture was a model to emulate.)

Now if we want to look for the roots of a *destructive* "modernity"—the ideology, say, of technocentrism and ecological degradation—we might start by looking in the project of "improvement," the subordination of all human values to productivity and profit rather than in the Enlightenment. Might we say that it is no accident that the mad cow disease scandal happened in Britain, the birthplace of "improvement"?

As we all know, it has become the height of fashion to attack the so-called Enlightenment project. The Enlightenment values enumerated earlier are supposed to be—and this is one of the milder indictments—"at the root of the disasters that have racked humanity throughout this century," everything from world wars and imperialism to ecological destruction.[4] This is not the place to pursue all the latest nonsense, by now far exceeding the reasonable insights that may once have been contained in critiques of the Enlightenment. The important point is that we are being invited to jettison all that is best in the Enlightenment project—especially its commitment to a universal human emancipation—and to blame these values for destructive effects we should be ascribing to capitalism. There are, then, many reasons, intellectual and political, for separating out the Enlightenment project from those aspects of our current condition that overwhelmingly belong not to the "project of modernity" but to capitalism.

Postmodernity

As commonly used, the concept of modernity breaks down some essential distinctions between social and cultural forms that do belong to capitalism and those that do not. In its tendency to conflate *bourgeois* with *capitalist*, it belongs to the standard view of history that takes capitalism for granted as the outcome of already existing tendencies, even natural laws, when and where they are given a chance. In the evolutionary process leading from early forms of exchange to modern industrial capitalism, modernity kicks in when these shackled economic forces and bourgeois economic rationality are liberated from traditional constraints. And so, *modernity* equals *bourgeois society* equals *capitalism*.

This concept of modernity has recently been supplemented with the idea of *post*-modernity. The postmodern epoch has been variously described, but always in relation to modernity. Postmodernity generally represents a phase of capitalism marked by certain distinctive economic and technological characteristics (the "information age," lean production, "flexible accumulation," "disorganized capitalism," consumerism, and so on). But, more particularly, it is marked by certain cultural formations summed up in the formula, "postmodern*ism*," whose single most outstanding feature is its challenge to the "Enlightenment project."

Postmodernism is said to have replaced the culture of modernism and the intellectual patterns associated with the "project of modernity." The project of modernity, according to these accounts, seems to have begun in the eighteenth century, or at least its defining moment was the Enlightenment, though it came to fruition in the nineteenth century. The so-called Enlightenment project is, again, supposed to represent rationalism, technocentrism, the standardization of knowledge and production, a belief in linear progress, and in universal, absolute truths. *Post*-modernism is understood as a reaction to that project—though it can also be seen as rooted in modernism, in the skepticism and sensitivity to change and contingency which are associated with certain twentieth-century cultural forms but which were already present in the Enlightenment. Postmodernism sees the world as essentially fragmented and indeterminate, rejects any "totalizing" discourses, any "metanarratives," any comprehensive and universalistic theories about the world and history. It also rejects any universalistic political projects, even universalistic emancipatory projects—in other words, projects for a general *human* emancipation rather than very particular struggles against very diverse and particular oppressions.

Some theories of postmodernity have been very illuminating, telling us much about capitalism in the late twentieth century and especially about its cultural forms.[5] But the concept itself is, in essence, an inversion of "modernity" in its conventional meaning and carries with it many of the same problematic presuppositions. This modernity belongs to a view of history that *cuts across* the great divide between capitalist and non-capitalist societies, a view that treats specifically capitalist laws of motion as if they were the universal laws of history and lumps together various very different historical developments, capitalist and non-capitalist. The idea of postmodernity is derived from a conception of modernity that, at its worst, makes capitalism historically invisible or, at the very least, *naturalizes* it.

It is important to notice, too, that even the *critique* of modernity can have the same effect of naturalizing capitalism. This effect was already visible long before today's postmodernist fashions, for instance in the sociological theories of Weber, specifically his theory of rationalization. The process of rationalization—the progress of reason and freedom associated with the Enlightenment—had, according to Weber, liberated humanity from traditional constraints. But at the same time, rationalization had produced and disguised a new oppression, the "iron cage" of modern organizational forms. There is, of course, much to be said for acknowledging the two sides of "modernity," not only the advances it is said to represent but also the destructive possibilities inherent in its productive capacities, its technologies, and its organizational forms—even in its universalistic values. But in an argument like Weber's, there is something more going on. Capitalism, like bureaucratic domination, is just a natural extension of the long-term progress of reason and freedom. It is worth noting, too, that in Weber we find something closely akin to the postmodernist ambivalence toward capitalism, in which lament is never very far away from celebration.

So *postmodernity* follows a *modernity* in which *bourgeois* is identical with *capitalist*, and Enlightenment *rationalism* is indistinguishable from the economic *rationality* of capitalism. These equations unavoidably entail some familiar assumptions about the origin of capitalism, especially that capitalism is already present in bourgeois rationality, just waiting for the moment of release. The idea of postmodernity certainly focuses our attention on historical transformations *within* capitalism, but it does so by disguising the transformations *between* capitalist and non-capitalist societies. The specificity of capitalism is again lost in the continuities of history, and the capitalist system is naturalized in the inevitable progress of the eternally rising bourgeoisie.

Conclusion

THIS BOOK HAS BEEN ABOUT THE ORIGIN OF CAPITALISM. WHAT does that origin tell us about the nature of the system itself?

First, it reminds us that capitalism is not a natural and inevitable consequence of human nature, or even of the age-old social tendency to "truck, barter, and exchange." It is a late and localized product of very specific historical conditions. The expansionary drive of capitalism, reaching a point of virtual universality today, is not the consequence of its conformity to human nature or to some transhistorical law but the product of its own historically specific internal laws of motion. And those laws of motion required vast social transformations and upheavals to set them in train. It required a transformation in the human metabolism with nature, in the provision of life's basic necessities.

Second, capitalism has, from the beginning, been a deeply contradictory force. We need only consider the most obvious effects of English agrarian capitalism: the conditions for material prosperity existed in early modern England as nowhere else, yet those conditions were achieved at the cost of widespread dispossession and intense exploitation. These new conditions also established the foundation and seeds for new and more effective forms of colonial expansion and imperialism in search of new markets, labor forces, and resources.

Then there are the corollaries of "improvement": productivity and the ability to feed a vast population set against the subordination of all other considerations to the imperatives of profit. This means, among other things, that people who could be fed are often left to starve. There is, in general, a great disparity between the productive capacities of capitalism and the quality of life it delivers. The ethic of "improvement" in its original sense, in which production is inseparable from profit, is also the ethic of exploitation, poverty, and homelessness.

Irresponsible land use and environmental destruction are also consequences of the ethic of productivity for profit. Capitalism was born at the very core of human life, in the interaction with nature on which life itself depends, and the transformation of that interaction by agrarian capitalism revealed the inherently destructive impulses of a system in which the very fundamentals of existence are subjected to the requirements of profit. In other words, the origin of capitalism revealed the essential secret of capitalism.

The expansion of capitalist imperatives throughout the world has regularly reproduced effects that it had at the beginning within its country of origin: dispossession, extinction of customary property rights, the imposition of market imperatives, and environmental destruction. These processes have extended their reach from the relations between exploiting and exploited classes to the relations between imperialist and subordinate countries. For example, more recently, in a new kind of imperialism, the spread of market imperatives (with the help of international capitalist agencies like the World Bank and the IMF) has compelled farmers in the third world to replace agricultural self-sufficiency with specialization in cash crops for the global market.

But if the destructive effects of capitalism have constantly reproduced themselves, its positive effects have not been nearly as consistent since the system's moment of origin. Once capitalism was established in one country, once it began to impose its imperatives on the rest of Europe and ultimately the whole world, its development in other places could never follow the same course as it had in its place of origin. The existence of one capitalist society thereafter transformed all others, and the subsequent expansion of capitalist imperatives constantly changed the conditions of economic development.

There is also a more general lesson to be drawn from the experience of English agrarian capitalism. Once market imperatives set the terms of social reproduction, all economic actors—both appropriators and producers, even if they remain in possession, or indeed outright ownership, of the means of production—are subject to the demands of competition, increasing productivity, capital accumulation, and the intense exploitation of labor.

For that matter, even the absence of a division between appropriators and producers is no guarantee of immunity. Once the market is established as an economic "discipline" or "regulator," once economic actors become market-dependent for the conditions of their own reproduction, even workers who own the means of production, individually or collectively, will be obliged to respond to the market's imperatives—to compete and accumulate, to let "uncompetitive" enterprises and their workers go to the wall, and to exploit themselves. The history of agrarian capitalism, and everything that followed from it, should make it clear that wherever market imperatives regulate the economy and govern social reproduction, there will be no escape from exploitation. There can, in other words, be no such thing as a truly "social" or democratic market, let alone a "market socialism."

I vividly remember—though the historic days of the Communist collapse now seem very distant—how idealistic democrats in the former Soviet Union and Eastern Europe responded to warnings about the market from the Western left (at a time when there still seemed to be an anti-market left in the West, and still some chance of dialogue between that left and more progressive forces in the former Communist countries). When people warned that the market means not only supermarkets with vast quantities and varieties of consumer goods but also mass unemployment and poverty, the reply would be, "Yes, of course, but that's not what we mean by the market." The idea was that you could pick and choose what you want from the self-regulating market. The market can act as a regulator of the economy just enough to guarantee some rationality, some correspondence between what people want and what is produced. The market can act as a signal, a source of information, a form of communication between consumers and producers, and it can guarantee that useless or inefficient enterprises will shape up or fall. But we can dispense with its nastier side.

All this no doubt seems as naive to many Russians and Eastern Europeans now as it did to some Western Marxists then, but the irony is that many on the Western left today are inclined to think that the market as an economic regulator is amenable to choice between its beneficent disciplines and its more destructive consequences. It is difficult to explain in any other way the notion of "market socialism," that contradiction in terms, or even the less utopian conception of the "social market," in which the market's ravages can be controlled by state regulation and an enhancement of social rights.

This is not to say that a social market is no better than unchecked free market capitalism. Nor does it mean that some institutions and practices associated with the market could not be adapted to a socialist economy. But we cannot refuse to confront the implications of the one irreducible condition without which the market cannot act as an economic discipline: the market dependence of direct producers, and specifically its most extreme form, the commodification of labor power—a condition which places the strictest limits on the "socialization" of the market and its capacity to assume a human face.[1]

Today it is more obvious than ever that the imperatives of the market will not allow capital to prosper without depressing the conditions of great multitudes of people and degrading the environment throughout the world. We have now reached the point where the destructive effects of capitalism are outstripping its material gains. No third world country today, for example, can hope to achieve even the contradictory development that England underwent. With the pressures of competition, accumulation, and exploitation imposed by more developed capitalist economies, and with the inevitable crises of overcapacity engendered by capitalist competition, the attempt to achieve material prosperity according to capitalist principles is increasingly likely to bring with it only the negative side of the capitalist contradiction, its dispossession and destruction without its material benefits—certainly for the vast majority.

As capitalism spreads more widely and penetrates more deeply into every aspect of social life and the natural environment, its contradictions are increasingly escaping all our efforts to control them. The hope of achieving a humane, truly democratic, and ecologically sustainable capitalism is becoming transparently unrealistic. But while that alternative is unavailable, there still remains the true alternative of socialism.

NOTES

Introduction

1. In my book, *The Pristine Culture of Capitalism: A Historical Essay on Old Regimes and Modern States* (London: Verso, 1991), I called this model of history the "bourgeois paradigm."

Chapter One

1. Henri Pirenne's most famous work was *Mohammed and Charlemagne* (London: Allen and Unwin, 1956), but a general summary of his whole thesis can be found in a series of his lectures, *Medieval Cities: The Origins and the Revival of Trade* (Princeton: Princeton University Press, 1969).

2. I discuss at some length the ways in which Weber adheres to the commercialization model in *Democracy Against Capitalism: Renewing Historical Materialism* (Cambridge: Cambridge University Press, 1995), chap. 5.

3. Robert Brenner makes this point in "Agrarian Class Structure and Economic Development in Pre-Industrial Europe," in *The Brenner Debate: Agrarian Class Structure and Economic Development in Pre-Industrial Europe,* eds. T. H. Aston and C. H. E. Philpin (Cambridge: Cambridge University Press, 1985), 10.

4. Perry Anderson, "Maurice Thomson's War," *London Review of Books*, 4 November 1993, 17.

5. Among the most prominent "revisionist" historians of England are Conrad Russell and John Morrill.

6. Michael Mann, *The Sources of Social Power,* vol. I (Cambridge: Cambridge University Press, 1986), 373.

7. Ibid., 374.

8. Karl Polanyi, *The Great Transformation* (Boston: Beacon Press, 1957), and George Dalton ed., *Primitive, Archaic, and Modern Economies: Essays of Karl Polanyi* (Boston: Beacon Press, 1971). The following quotations are all taken from the former.

9. Polanyi, 76.

10. Ibid., 42.

11. Ibid., 41.

12. Ibid., 40.

13. Ibid., 33.

14. Ibid., 37.

15. Ibid.

16. Daniel R. Fusfield, "The Market in History," *Monthly Review* 45 (May 1993): 6.

Chapter Two

1. On the two theories of history in Marx, see George Comninel, *Rethinking the French Revolution: Marxism and the Revisionist Challenge* (London: Verso, 1987). See also Robert Brenner, "Bourgeois Revolution and Transition to Capitalism," in *The First Modern Society,* ed. A. L. Beier and others (Cambridge: Cambridge University Press, 1989).

2. R. H. Hilton, ed., *The Transition from Feudalism to Capitalism* (London: Verso, 1976).

3. Maurice Dobb in ibid., 59.

4. Hilton in ibid., 27.

5. Paul Sweezy in ibid., 49.

6. Ibid., 54.

7. Ibid., 106-7.

8. Ibid.

9. Brenner, "The Origins of Capitalist Development: A Critique of Neo-Smithian Marxism," *New Left Review* 104 (July-August 1977): 25-92.

10. See, for example, Hilton in *Transition,* 157-59.

11. Perry Anderson, *Lineages of the Absolutist State* (London: Verso, 1974), 19.

12. Ibid.

13. Ibid., 23.

14. Ibid., 18.

15. Anderson, "Maurice Thomson's War," *London Review of Books,* 4 November 1993, 17.

16. See, for example, Karl Marx, *Capital,* vol. 1 (Moscow, n.d.), 699-701.

17. Brenner, "The Origins of Capitalist Development": 76-77.

Chapter Three

1. Brenner's original article was first published in *Past and Present* 70 (February 1976). Responses from M. M. Postan and

John Hatcher, Patricia Croot and David Parker, Heide Wunder, Emmanuel Le Roy Ladurie, Guy Bois, R. H. Hilton, J. P. Cooper, and Arnost Klima followed in subsequent issues, with a comprehensive reply from Brenner at the end. The whole debate was republished in T. H. Aston and C. H. E. Philpin, eds., *The Brenner Debate: Agrarian Class Structure and Economic Development in Pre-Industrial Europe* (Cambridge: Cambridge University Press, 1985). Brenner's other most important works are "The Origins of Capitalist Development: A Critique of Neo-Smithian Marxism," *New Left Review* 104 (July-August 1977): 25-92; "The Social Basis of Economic Development," in *Analytical Marxism,* ed. John Roemer (Cambridge: Cambridge University Press, 1985); "Bourgeois Revolution and Transition to Capitalism," in *The First Modern Society,* ed. A. L. Beier and others (Cambridge: Cambridge University Press, 1989); and *Merchants and Revolution: Commercial Change, Political Conflict, and London's Overseas Traders, 1550-1653* (Princeton: Princeton University Press, 1993).

2. See, for example, Robert Albritton, "Did Agrarian Capitalism Exist?" *Journal of Peasant Studies* 20 (April 1993: 419-41.

3. For example, Brian Manning's review of Brenner's *Merchants and Revolution:* "The English Revolution and the transition from feudalism to capitalism," *International Socialism* 63 (Summer 1994): 84.

4. Ibid., 82.

5. Perry Anderson, "Maurice Thomson's War," *London Review of Books,* 4 November 1993, 17.

6. Brenner, "Bourgeois Revolution and Transition to Capitalism." For an earlier statement of a similar argument, see George Comninel, *Rethinking the French Revolution: Marxism and the Revisionist Challenge* (London: Verso, 1987).

7. Brenner, "Bourgeois Revolution": 280.

8. I have discussed this point at greater length in *The Pristine Culture of Capitalism* (London: Verso, 1991).

9. See, for example, G. A. Cohen, *Karl Marx's Theory of History: A Defence* (Princeton: Princeton University Press, 1978), 75; and Perry Anderson, *Arguments Within English Marxism* (London: Verso, 1980), 40.

10. E. P. Thompson, *The Making of the English Working Class* (Harmondsworth: Penguin, 1963), 288-89. See also 222-23.

11. Thompson, *Customs in Common* (London: Merlin, 1991), 38-42.

Chapter Four

1. I have sketched out this argument about the path from Graeco-Roman antiquity to Western feudalism and, beyond that, to capitalism, in the first chapter of my book *Democracy Against Capitalism: Renewing Historical Materialism* (Cambridge: Cambridge University Press, 1995), especially 31-39. I also outline the distinctiveness of ancient Roman property forms, and their implications for later developments in Western Europe, 250-52. There are some very tentative speculations about the Greek origins of Western property forms in my *Peasant-Citizen and Slave: The Foundations of Athenian Democracy* (London: Verso, 1988), especially 91-92. On the specificity of property relations in Greek and Roman antiquity, see also *Democracy Against Capitalism*, 187-90.

2. I develop parts of this argument about the different outcomes of European feudalism, especially with respect to English capitalism and French absolutism, in *The Pristine Culture of Capitalism* (London: Verso, 1991).

3. Eric Kerridge, *Trade and Banking in Early Modern England* (Manchester: Manchester University Press, 1988), 6.

4. This discussion of the particularities of English property relations is, of course, deeply indebted to Robert Brenner, and especially to his two articles in T. H. Aston and C. H. E. Philpin, eds., *The Brenner Debate* (Cambridge: Cambridge University Press, 1985).

5. John Merrington, "Town and Country in the Transition to Capitalism," in *The Transition from Feudalism to Capitalism*, ed. R. H. Hilton (London: Verso, 1976), 179.

6. On regulation of production by the peasant community in France, see the conclusion of George Comninel, *Rethinking the French Revolution: Marxism and the Revisionist Challenge* (London: Verso, 1987).

7. On these early social critics, see Neal Wood, *The Foundations of Political Economy: Some Early Tudor Views on State and Society,* (Berkeley and Los Angeles: University of California Press, 1994).

8. See E. P. Thompson, "Custom, Law and Common Right" in *Customs in Common* (London: Merlin, 1991).

9. The discussion on Locke that follows here is drawn from the chapter on Locke in Ellen Meiksins Wood and Neal Wood, *A Trumpet of Sedition: Political Theory and the Rise of Capitalism, 1509-1688* (London and New York: New York University Press, 1997). For a detailed discussion of Locke and the "improvement" literature of the seventeenth century, see Neal Wood, *John Locke and Agrarian Capitalism* (Berkeley and Los Angeles: University of California Press, 1984).

10. I am indebted for this point about Petty to a doctoral dissertation, still in progress, by Cathy Livingstone, York University, Toronto, Canada.

11. On the French Revolution and the state as a major material issue, see Comninel, *Rethinking the French Revolution,* especially the concluding chapter.

12. See Wood and Wood, *Trumpet of Sedition,* especially Chapter Four, on this radical legacy.

Chapter Five

1. See E. J. Hobsbawm, *The Age of Empire* (London: Weidenfeld and Nicholson, 1987), 343.

2. On the lack of "improvement" in French agriculture in the seventeenth century and throughout much of the eighteenth, see Hugues Neveux, Jean Jacquart, and Emmanuel Le Roy Ladurie, *L'age classique des paysans, 1340-1789* (Paris: Editions du Seuil, 1975), especially 214-15. It is worth adding that French landlords did not regard their tenants as entrepreneurs or improvers. See Robert Forster, "Obstacles to Agricultural Growth in Eighteenth-Century France," *American Historical Review* 75 (1970): 1610.

3. The one case most commonly cited as England's rival in the race to capitalism, at least in its early phases (though it counts as a "failed transition" in the development of industrial capitalism), the early modern Dutch Republic, represents an interesting contrast here. An important trading power with a well-developed commercial agriculture as well as a rich urban society, its prosperous peasants, in contrast to peasants elsewhere, did constitute a market for certain luxury goods, but it never produced the kind of mass market for cheap everyday goods that developed in England. It would be interesting to speculate on what this tells about property relations in the Republic. At any rate, it has been argued that the very characteristics which the commercialization model treats as the motors of economic development—flourishing cities and international trade—proved in the Dutch case to be major factors in *blocking* further development. See, for example, Jan de Vries, *The Dutch Rural Economy in the Golden Age, 1500-1700* (New Haven: Yale University Press, 1974). According to this argument, the Republic's powerful cities eventually strangled

Dutch productivity by imposing upon it a rentier-type parasitism which acted as a drain on its flourishing agriculture. At the same time, dependence on the traditional international trading system subjected the Republic to a European economic crisis in the seventeenth century to which England alone remained immune—not least because of England's internal market and its "capitalism in one country."

4. Eric Kerridge, *Trade and Banking in Early Modern England* (Manchester: Manchester University Press, 1988), 4-6.

5. Ibid., 6.

6. The Marxist classics on this subject are the works of Eric Williams, *Capitalism and Slavery* (New York: Russell and Russell, 1961) and C. L. R. James, *The Black Jacobins* (New York: Vintage, 1989). The most recent major contribution to this debate is Robin Blackburn's *The Making of New World Slavery* (London: Verso, 1997).

7. Blackburn makes this argument.

8. I discuss the development of other European capitalisms in response to competitive pressures emanating from England in *The Pristine Culture of Capitalism* (London: Verso, 1991), especially 103-106.

9. See Eric Hobsbawm, *Industry and Empire* (New York: Pantheon, 1968).

Chapter Six

1. I discuss these cultural and intellectual expressions of French absolutism in *The Pristine Culture of Capitalism* (London: Verso, 1991).

2. Marshall Berman, *All That is Solid Melts into Air: The Experience of Modernity* (New York: Simon and Schuster, 1982), 18.

3. See Wood, *Pristine Culture,* for more on this contrast between the culture of English capitalism and French absolutism.

4. Roger Burbach, "For a Zapatista Style Postmodernist Perspective," *Monthly Review* 47 (March 1996): 37.

5. See, for instance, David Harvey, *The Condition of Postmodernity* (Oxford and Cambridge, Mass.: Blackwell, 1989) and Fredric Jameson, *Postmodernism, or, The Cultural Logic of Late Capitalism* (London: Verso, 1991).

Conclusion

1. For a critique of the market and its dependence on the commodification of labor power, see David McNally, *Against the Market* (London: Verso, 1993), especially Chapter 6.

Index